'Laugh along with the indominatible Jo as she stands surreptitiously turning light switches on and off, intrigued that they actually make a noise, weep with admiration at her amazing family, and wish you could aim a swift kick at the backside of a heartless lecturer, one of a long list of idiots who thoughtlessly attempt to humiliate an extraordinary woman.'   Jojo Moyes

'A quietly devastating book about disability . . . These stories should shame us all. Yet, ultimately, her book will inspire us. Jo is a remarkable woman and a wonderful writer, and Breaking the Silence demands to be widely read.'   *Mail on Sunday*

'An incredibly moving and inspiring story.'   *The Journal*

'Her memoir of a life lived in light and darkness, silence and sound, is bright with her courage and humanity.'   *The Times*

'A fascinating insight into the challenge of living with a disability, but also a sobering reminder of the prejudice that people with disabilities routinely face.'   *The Scotsman*

'If 31 million people have been drawn to the emotion of Milne's switch-on, that is only half the story.'   *Times Magazine*

'Extremely moving.'   *The Sunday Express*

04401368

BREAKING
THE SILENCE

**My journey of discovery
as I heard for the very first time**

Jo Milne

CORONET

First published in Great Britain in 2015 by Coronet
An imprint of Hodder & Stoughton
An Hachette UK company

First published in paperback in 2016

1

Copyright © Jo Milne 2016

The right of Jo Milne to be identified as the Author of the Work has been asserted
by *him/her* in accordance with the Copyright, Designs and Patents Act 1988.

A CIP catalogue record for this title is available from the British Library

Paperback ISBN: 9781473606036
Ebook ISBN: 9781473606029

Typeset by Hewer Text UK Ltd, Edinburgh

Printed and bound by Clays Ltd, St Ives plc

Hodder & Stoughton policy is to use papers that are natural, renewable and recyclable
products and made from wood grown in sustainable forests. The logging and manufacturing
processes are expected to conform to the environmental regulations of the country of origin.

Hodder & Stoughton Ltd
Carmelite House
50 Victoria Embankment
London EC4Y 0DZ

www.hodder.co.uk

I dedicate *Breaking the Silence* to my 'ever-loving Granddad', as he called himself. The man who always had a smile, and a 'deep belly laugh' for all his grandchildren. Who gave me hours and hours of his time through speech therapy and patience. Every single child deserves to feel they can do anything and there are no limits to one's capability with the right guidance and support. His wise words have been instilled in me to be the person I am today... to always have respect for others and their differences and 'Do unto others as you would have them do unto you'.

'It's nice, to be nice.'
William Edward Moore 1913 – 2000

In addition to my Grandfather's memory, I know he would not mind sharing this dedication with all those with hidden disabilities, particularly sensory loss and Usher Syndrome.

'Kindness is the language which the deaf can hear and the blind can see.' (Mark Twain)

Standing at a bus stop, a woman approaches me. She tries to speak to me, over-pronouncing each of her words into loud, long indistinguishable vowels.

She can tell I don't understand, but she doesn't give up. She gesticulates, pointing to her ears, mouthing: 'I'm deaf.'

I look into her eyes and I know she's needs something from me, but I'm feeling hot with discomfort. I don't understand.

I smile and shrug, then walk away.

It's only after I leave the bus stop that I realise, all she wanted was the time. How easy would it have been to just roll up my sleeve and show her my wrist watch?

The guilt washes over me, but I carry on walking. . . .

Jo's mum, 1969.

Prologue

I'm sitting on a busy train. You might have spotted me, but chances are I haven't noticed you.

You might even have hovered over me for a split second deciding whether to sit next to me, before choosing another seat a few rows ahead. Not that I realised.

You saw a woman with a white stick, a guide dog. Yet, I didn't even hear your footsteps approaching me or walking away.

This is the deafblind world I live in. A silent world interrupted only by white noise, a world that's black around the edges pin sharp in the middle.

Imagine shining a torch directly ahead of you in a pitch black night. That's what I see, the bright bit lighting up the way ahead. Or perhaps to you, it would be like peering through a letterbox, or the wrong way down a pair of binoculars – a perfect view in the centre, but completely black around the edges.

My window onto the world is getting smaller and smaller all the time, the world around me is getting darker with each day, the tunnel more narrow. Who knows if tomorrow I'll wake up and be able to see anything on this train?

Instead, for now, if I want to look down, I move my head. See, there's the floor. I look to my right and spot a pair of legs swinging from the seat. A child. I move my head up and there are her knees, her tummy, her arms, her pigtails. She's laughing. Silently to me, of course.

My thoughts are interrupted by the brush of someone sitting down next to me, a waft of cool air. I can feel their body, but I can't see them, can't hear them. They are in the dark, in my dark. Is it a man or a woman? I'll have to wait for clues.

I feel the vibration as they shuffle a newspaper in their hands. I can smell coffee too, is it theirs? I quickly tell myself to be careful in case there's a hot drink nearby. Their arm is relaxing lightly against mine, the warmth of their body starting to radiate through my coat.

Have they spoken to me? I wouldn't know. I hope I didn't appear rude by not answering if they did. Instead, I conjure up a picture in my mind of the two of us sitting side by side.

I look to the floor and spot a pair of brown leather shoes. Men's shoes. It's a man beside me.

I look ahead trying to piece together an image of the other people in my carriage. I feel my guide dog, Matt, shuffle on the floor by my feet.

I smell a strong, sweet perfume. You perhaps wouldn't notice. You might be too busy chatting on your mobile phone, or reading a newspaper like the man beside me. But I sit and smile, filling in the blanks of my missing picture, like a detective waiting for the next clue.

The perfume must belong to a woman who's about to meet her boyfriend, I tell myself. Or perhaps she has a first date. I can't see her unless I look up, down, around the carriage, even then I might not be able to spot her. But I know she's there.

Then I hear something, but not like you hear. Among the white noise, my mind's constant companion, I hear a low, vibrato sound. A deep hum, one of the only 'sounds' I can pick up with my hearing aids. Perhaps that's why a deep belly laugh is one of my favourites – it's one of the few things I can distinguish.

I picture its owner, eyes creased, clutching his tummy as his arms bob up and down at his sides, his shoulders shaking as he attempts to stifle his laughs. Has he read something funny? Is he on the phone to one of his children?

I can't hear anyone talking in the carriage, perhaps a low hum among the white noise, but if anyone was speaking to me, I wouldn't know.

This is my life as a deafblind woman. I'd long to speak to each and every person in this carriage. I'd love to make eye contact and smile, to ask them about their day and chat about mine. But instead I sit, trapped in my darkened, silent world, peering out through my letterbox...

But soon that might all change. It is a month before my operation. The surgeons are confident that a cochlea implant has a good chance of working for me. That one day I might be able to hear that belly laugh for real, or listen to that little girl giggle for the first time. Perhaps I could even eavesdrop on the girl spritzed with perfume, gossiping excitedly on the phone to her friend about the man she's about to meet.

How would that feel? What would it be like to fill my silent world with so many different sounds? Will it work?

Could it be that at forty years-old the world will suddenly turn up its volume and let me in? I'm scared because it could also go so wrong, stripping me of even the white noise that I've come to rely on so much.

Instead, I ignore the fear and turn to the window. Bright sunshine streams in through the glass, flooding my tunnel vision with plain, white light...

Chapter One

I'm sixteen months old and sitting in front of the fire in our living room on our brown shag pile rug. I like the way the wool tickles between my bare pink toes. I giggle and try to catch the threads between my fat fingers; my feet wiggle as I do and it only tickles me more. I chuckle to myself.

I know this room so well: the orange-and-coffee-coloured swirly wool carpet; the fashionable seventies brick fireplace; the sage green and tangerine feature walls that Mam painted when she and Dad first moved into this place, seven years before I was born. They were newlyweds back then; they'd moved out of the city of Newcastle, where they'd both grown up, and into this new estate in Gateshead. The brown brick semi-detached houses were all brand new, staggered up and down the steep street surrounded by picture-perfect countryside. It must have seemed like a flash new place then, especially compared to the terraced streets that they'd grown up in. The Chowdene estate in Low Fell where they bought their first-ever home consisted of streets bearing the names of English coastal towns: Weymouth, Dartmouth, Frome, Cromer, St. Austell. Newly planted cherry trees lined the avenue; there was a garden at the front and at the back, and even a garage for their white Morris car.

Mam and Dad were soon joined by plenty of other young couples all fleeing the grey industrial city for a green view, rolling fields and somewhere lovely to bring up the children. Many of the new residents – like Mam and Dad – stayed childless for the first few years of their marriage, enjoying all the fun the late sixties and early seventies had to afford them. They saw The Beatles at Newcastle's Majestic Hall, spent the weekends at gigs with friends, and flooded their record player with the music of Elvis, Cliff Richard and the Everly Brothers.

My parents were rock and rollers in the early sixties. The night they met, at a dance at the Majestic, Mam wore a white Mary Quant-style dress that she'd made and appliquéd with big purple flowers. Her light blonde hair was styled into a beehive and held there with lashings of hairspray. In the years to come, Mam would tell me and my sisters countless times how she fell for my dad, who worked as a plater in the shipyards on the River Tyne back then. She was swept away by his blue showaddywaddy-style drapes trimmed with velvet, and his hair styled with Brylcreem into the typical teddy-boy bunch of grapes on his forehead. She thought he looked so handsome. They must have looked great, the pair of them. Young, carefree, hip and trendy.

They'd bought that first house for £3,600 – a lot of money in those days – and somehow scraped together a £600 deposit, despite the fact they took home less than £10 a week between them. They were both working; Mam as a secretary for a chemical company, while Dad eventually moved to Caterpillar, not far from our house.

And that house was soon to be busier than ever. As the rock and roll era rolled on by, pregnancies spread up and down our street like the lobelia that my parents had newly planted in their flowerbeds. No sooner had Mam told a neighbour she was expecting our Julie, someone two doors down was sharing the same exciting news of her own. The women must have waddled up and down the sloping street for much of the early seventies. Soon the sound of rock and roll on record players was replaced by the cries of newborn babies as everyone settled down to start their families, and the washing lines seemingly filled up with bright white terry-towelling nappies overnight.

Dad wasn't around much in those days. He worked away, laying electrical cable at nuclear power plants like Sellafield and Torness. The money was good, but it came at a cost: being away from his family all week.

Mam's dad, Bill – Granddad – was around more than Dad in the week. His wife Doris – my grandma – had died before I was born, so he'd come over to our house every Monday for Mam's mince and dumplings. He'd jiggle me up and down on his knee and help Julie practise her reading while Mam mashed up a portion with a fork for me. I'd only turned one a few months before; my sister Julie was four. With nearly four years between us we looked alike with our matching blonde hair. I often give Julie's a tug when she's wearing one of her enticing bunches and watch her face screw up in irritation. Julie often runs around and dances in our living room; it makes me laugh every time she does, toppling over onto our swirly carpet.

She is skipping around out in the back garden now, while Mam and Dad sit perched on the edge of our brown furry sofa behind me. They put me down on the rug a few minutes ago. My back is to them, but I know they're still there. Not because I can hear them, but every so often I feel the vibrations of their feet shuffling on the carpet. Little giveaway signs like that have become second nature to me, almost subconscious.

I'm oblivious to the experiment they're carrying out behind me as I reach for a few discarded stickle bricks in front of the fireplace.

First they call my name. '*Joanne . . .*'

Then louder: '*Joanne!*'

But of course I don't turn round.

Next they clap. Again, nothing. Louder still . . . I don't so much as turn my head. Mam tries leaning forward from the sofa, clapping close to one side of my head, then the other. I don't even flinch. Dad tries a louder clap with his big hands. Nothing. Instead, I stay staring at the coloured stickle bricks on the floor in front of me: blue, green, red. My eyes dart, delighted, between the colours, instead of seeing the worried looks Mam and Dad are exchanging between them right now.

I'm oblivious to the fact that Mam has her head in her hands, that she's telling Dad she always had a feeling that something wasn't 'quite right', but it had taken Mrs Cain next door to suggest to her that I was deaf. How she'd waited all week for Dad to come home from work to tell him.

Dad tries again. *Clap*. No reaction.

Mam is telling Dad how it's taken me longer to learn words than it did Julie. Dad tries to tell her that all children develop at different times. Mam knows that. But this is different. She's telling him how I was trying to say the word 'elephant' the other week. But no matter how many times she repeated it, I couldn't grasp the sound. Instead I copied her mouth, sticking my tongue out to make an 'l', but with no idea what the word *sounded* like.

But it's a difficult word, Dad is saying.

She knows that, too, but it was just a feeling, an instinct. Something wasn't right.

And then came that day in the garden – just a few days ago – when Mrs Cain had offered me a sweetie over the garden fence and I hadn't responded. Unlike most other kids my age, I hadn't toddled over to take it from her hand.

'I think your Joanne might be deaf,' she'd told Mam, confirming her worst fears. It was the first time that anyone else had said it.

Now, while I chew on a yellow stickle brick, they're talking about all the times they've called my name, how they've sung to me, and read me bedtime stories. Now it's sinking in that I never heard a word. My smiles were simply because I delighted in the pictures they were pointing at in the books; I was happy because I was snuggled up under their arm, that I had their one-hundred-per-cent attention. I eventually giggled when I was grumpy because I loved their faces, the dance of their eyes, not because I could hear their voices soothing me.

Perhaps that's why I always cry when Mam leaves the room, Dad is suggesting, it makes sense if I can't hear her pottering in the kitchen, or calling out to me from the cooker. Most babies feel reassured when their mam goes next door to make a cup of tea; she might be gone from their sight, but they know she's still there from the sounds. Except I didn't. To me, Mam was gone. I couldn't hear her reassuring calls to me, her humming as she made up a bottle of milk. I was plunged into silence. All colour from my life faded away. A once-warm room suddenly turned cold without Mam smiling at me from the sofa, or tickling my toes as I rocked in my yellow plastic baby bouncer, kicking my chubby legs and laughing.

The television that she told Julie to turn down was no bother to me, just a flash of interesting pictures that jumped in front of my eyes. No wonder I was such a good sleeper when Julie had been racing round the house as a toddler – I couldn't hear a thing, they're saying now.

But neither Mam nor Dad had realised until now that my world is a silent one. Why would they?

If I turned round now, I might see the worry etched across Mam's face, the look in her eyes that wonders why she hadn't noticed before. Had she been less attentive to me than she had Julie? How *could* she not have known? A mother and baby's bond is made up of more than just words though. Love is found in those silent gestures: a shared look, a swapped smile. All reassurance exchanged in a split second, just in a glance. Like a purr offered between cat and kitten.

Now they are talking about taking me to see doctors, specialists; about whether they should mention it to my health visitor. Oblivious, my chubby fingers reach for a red stickle brick on the carpet. I pick it up and start to chew on it.

Granddad is a military man. His father before him – my great-granddad – was too. Everything about Granddad is pristine. His white hair is always swept perfectly across to the right. His clothes are cleanly pressed, and he always smells of Imperial Leather soap. His shoes shine; his coat doesn't have so much as a stray hair on it. It might only be a Monday, and he's just round at ours for mince and dumplings, but Granddad hasn't skimped on style. He wears a suit and matching waistcoat. He leaves his hat and gloves in their familiar place on the dining table. But whatever the weather, he always comes to ours wearing his trademark smile. He has a round, happy face. His eyes crease at the sides when he sees us girls, and when he wraps me up in a big hug I feel so warm and safe. He's a no-nonsense man, yet he spoils us with chocolate bars, one for every day of the week. He delights in our smiles, rejoices in our giggles; now my grandma has left him, his grandchildren are everything.

His own father, William Moore, served in the military out in South Africa. He was stationed there with the British Army, dealing with the after-effects of the Boer War. It was there that William met his future wife, Johanna van Wyck, my grandfather's mother. She didn't speak any English, only Afrikaans Dutch. A bit like a Geordie woman from back home, she was strong and no-nonsense; she was a determined young woman and picked up English very quickly. She married my great-grandfather when she was just nineteen.

Granddad was born in Cape Town in 1913, and another brother and sister followed on after they were stationed in Johannesburg. They later moved to Gibraltar, where my great-grandfather was in charge of the cannons; there they had another child, a daughter. Each of these children had Johanna's trademark blonde hair and blue eyes, so typical of the Netherlands. Even me and Julie have Johanna van Wyck's fair features, so strong are her genes.

Granddad followed his father into the army, and rose to the ranks of sergeant major he was decorated for his bravery in the Second World War. He retired at sixty, and now he spends a lot of time here with us in our little house. On Mondays he sits around our teak dining table, the burgundy curtains drawn in the winter. Julie sits at the table next to Mam and me in my highchair, spooning mouthfuls of mashed potatoes into my mouth but getting most of it on my chin.

Even as a tiny tot I can see that Mam likes to have Granddad around. With Dad gone in the week he's the only father figure we know. A perfect mix of straight-talking and gentle words. He's security for all of us. And he's here now, as the man in the brown suit and glasses watches me play on the floor. I reach for a book and he hands it to me. A few minutes later, I've moved on to the crayons and pieces of paper that Mam's put down.

I don't know why this man – Mr Edgar – is here. Every so often, he'll say something to Mam, perhaps ask her a question. I watch his lips moving but, of course, I have no idea what he's saying. But I can feel Mam's anxiety. She takes deep breaths in and out, folds and unfolds her arms as he makes his appraisal of me. She tries to busy herself in the kitchen, but she keeps coming back, clutching a tea towel, to check if anything has happened. Granddad is the calming presence. The lifebuoy in the storm.

I play on the floor, oblivious to the attention I'm receiving. Not at all curious as to why this man – so official – is here in our living room. He's actually been sent here by my health visitor. After Mam and Dad had sat me on the floor a few days ago, they'd called and told her their fears. It was she who'd arranged for Mr Edgar to come.

He's here to assess whether I am in fact deaf. If he calls out to me, I don't notice. Perhaps he does other things like clapping or banging something on the table. He may have pulled something out of the brown briefcase that he's carrying to try to catch my attention. But, caught up in my colouring book on the carpet in silent concentration, I have no idea. And before I know it, he's standing up to leave.

Mam comes in to see him to the front door. I watch her search his face for clues, but I'm unaware of just how desperate she is for answers. I see him nodding. He tells her that yes, I am deaf. And inside she must have been crushed, but I wouldn't have found a clue written on her face, or in her voice had I heard it.

He's gone now, and Mam's in the kitchen with Granddad. Julie rushes in and quickly comes back out to watch the telly in the living room with me, while I pull myself up to standing and take some tentative steps along the side of the sofa. If I could toddle, should my legs be able to carry me, and I could make it to the kitchen now instead of surfing our brown settee, I might see that

Mam is worried, that Granddad is reassuring her. It might be impossible for her to hide the fear in her eyes from me – so adept are we both at reading each other's signals. She's telling Granddad that she's worried about how I'll cope, what about school? What about making friends? But with typical calmness and perfect sense Granddad is telling her that I'll be fine. He's reminding her that you take what God has given you and you get on with it – there is no choice.

Mam is nodding now. Granddad is kind but firm: this isn't a disaster. Mam nods more. There is no need for Joanne to be any different from Julie. People wear glasses if they can't see properly; if Joanne can't hear she'll wear a hearing aid, he's saying. If I were in the kitchen I'd see how Mam's relaxing a little more now, how her chest isn't heaving with fear, how her shoulders have relaxed down, how instead she's turning back to the cooker to serve up mince and dumplings. Her mind might be racing, but she knows Granddad is right. We'll deal with whatever is thrown our way, and we'll get on with it as a family.

Unaware of any of this adult conversation, I attempt a tentative step away from the furniture and towards Julie in the middle of the carpet, where she's watching television cross-legged. I fall down onto my bottom. My swollen terry-towelling nappy cushions the blow.

I'm sitting in front of a handful of marbles. I'm two years old by now. The glass marbles are full of pretty colours, swirls of yellow, blue and green. I pick one up and look into it, seeing the way the shape of the colour dances in front of my eyes as I roll the glass sphere between my fingers. The streak of pigment twists and turns through the turquoise-tinged hard ball. The light from the window shines through, picking out one of two tiny bubbles within the glass. I stare at them, mesmerised. As a toddler it's taking me all my strength not to pop one in my mouth right now. These marbles look like pretty, twinkly sweeties. So tempting.

But instead, Mr Mathias is kneeling down in front of me. He is wearing a suit and a friendly smile.

He moves directly in front of me so I can watch his lips. But of course, no sound accompanies them. His eyes are encouraging as he explains slowly, lifting one marble from the table, pointing to his ears and then putting it into a tub. Then he nods, smiles. Searches my face for any indication that I understand what he's saying.

I look up to Mam, who is standing beside me. She's wearing her lilac flares and a tight red T-shirt.

I remember watching her get dressed this morning, a distant look I didn't recognise in her eyes. She had turned and smiled at me, like she was trying hard to change the subject contained in the glances that passed between us.

But when we arrived at Dryden Road Children's Hospital, I noticed that she gripped my hand a little tighter than usual as we entered the huge red-brick Victorian building. She walked fast as she led me to the audiology department.

Everything seemed huge to tiny little me. High Victorian ceilings, long straight corridors, big sash windows and large metal light-fittings containing stark white light bulbs swinging above us.

The smell of disinfectant hit my nose and snaked its way up my nostrils. We passed other people as we made our way along the corridors: children bigger than me in wheelchairs, plaster casts; nurses in white crisp uniforms pushing them, their faces blank.

Not like Mr Mathias in front of me now, with his big friendly smile. Mam bends down and picks up another marble. Like Mr Mathias before her, she points to her ears, nods and then pops another marble into the tub. That's what they want me to do. When something happens in my ears.

I reach up to touch them, but the soft fleshy feel of my ears has been replaced by something hard and alien. I'm wearing a pair of heavy, black headphones. They push down on my small head, making my neck ache under the weight. My shoulders feel heavy.

This isn't comfortable. I wriggle; I want to take them off. But Mam and Mr Mathias put out their arms to steady me in my seat. Again they repeat: picking up a marble, pointing to my ears, nodding and placing it in the tub. And with that the test starts. Except I don't know it's a test to see exactly what my ears can pick up. To me it's a game. The noises are so loud in the headphones that Mam can hear their muffled echo as she stands beside me in the room.

If I looked up at her now, I might see her head gently jerking with each sound she heard, willing me to hear it too, to place a marble in the tub. But instead the marbles stay on the table in front of me. If I pick one up it's to marvel at the colour inside, not because I've heard anything. Look, there's a yellow one with a tiny brown fleck inside it. I hold it up to Mam to show her.

And then, there's something. It's coming through my ears, my head. A very low hum – is that what it is? I look up at Mam for reassurance, then I remember the instructions that have been repeated to me. I place a marble in the tub. Mam smiles, encouraging. I see her visibly relax. I smile back, I want to please her. As the test continues, a few more marbles end up in the tub. Who knows how many I placed in there just to make Mam smile? The nurses probably know that they're not in time with the range of sounds being played down my headphones. Instead, most of the high-pitched squeaks go without being registered by my small ears. Mam knows for certain then that her suspicions were right.

I am deaf.

Mr Mathias confirms it.

As the grown-ups start talking, I scan their faces to see if I did right. Are they pleased with me for putting the marbles in the tub? Can I take them out and play with them now? Again the temptation to pop one in my mouth washes over me, but I resist, because the adults are talking seriously now. Mam is listening as Mr Mathias is telling her that they believe I'm deaf, that the fact that I registered some of the low sounds meant they could fit me with hearing aids. This news seems to please Mam; she nods eagerly. I watch her shoulders relax.

When we leave the hospital a few minutes later, Mam's grip on my hand isn't as tight as when we went in. Her footsteps aren't so clipped. I skip alongside her as we head home to pick Julie up from school.

Mam knows she has a deaf child then, but the hearing aids will turn me into a hearing one. She's sure of that. I will be just like my friends, just like Julie.

Not that she wants me to be like everyone else. 'What a boring place the world would be if we were all born the same,' my grandma always used to tell her. She knows that, too.

But as we push open the heavy doors of the hospital and step into the July sunshine, she can't help but wonder: as a mother, isn't there always just a part of you that wants your children to be like all the others?

Chapter Two

Mam is very excited today. She's been dancing around the kitchen all morning, even though there's no music. You might wonder how a deaf child knows there's no music. My clue is that Julie doesn't dance along with her. Instead she stands beside me, giggling as Mam dances between the sink and the cooker, wiggling her hips and swaying from side to side.

When Mam's happy, so am I. I'm used to taking so many of my cues from her. In my silent world she is often my eyes and ears. Like many toddlers, if I'm unsure of anything, a quick glance towards Mam will put my mind at rest. But, for me, a reassuring look from Mam does more than that: it fills the silence in the room with warmth.

Right now, I'm kneeling on the floor of the waiting room at the Dryden Road Children's Hospital. There's an abacus sitting on a small table beside me. Since my diagnosis, this hospital waiting room – and this toy – have become a regular part of my life. Each time we arrive, I rush over to play with it, my tiny toddler fingers swishing the colourful beads this way and that. Sometimes I count too: one . . . two . . . three . . .

I spy another toy, a Fisher-Price Treehouse. The top of the tree pushes down and hides the house, but when you pop it up there's the kitchen and fold-down stairs. A little brown door with a round hole cut out that goes up and down from the bottom of the tree. There's even a doggie kennel outside, and a swing. I go over and put the little boy with yellow hair on the swing, give it a little push, and look up at Mam to check she's watching me play. She's humming to herself as she sits on the hard waiting-room chair. I can tell she's humming because her lips are closed tight, her foot taps up and down, and every so often I notice her chest heaving as she takes another deep breath in to exhale slowly through her nose. If Julie were here, she'd be dancing around now. She smiles encouragingly to me, then Mr Mathias's door opens. Mam gets up from her seat and beckons me to follow her. I toddle into his office behind her.

I like Mr Mathias. He's one of the few people who talk to me instead of just to Mam. Ever since we left the hospital a few weeks ago, after the marble test, I've noticed that some people don't speak to me so much anymore. Perhaps they wonder what the point is if I can't hear them. Not Mam and Dad, Granddad, Julie or friends, mostly strangers who might have heard word on the Chowdene estate and spot Mam out pushing me in my buggy.

My deaf diagnosis hasn't changed anything for Mam though. She reads and sings and talks to me like she always did. Only this morning as we went to the bus stop she was singing nursery rhymes to me all the way.

I can tell which one it is by the way she swings her arm, or the rhythm that she skips with her hand in mine. I skip happily alongside her singing away in time. I can't hear her voice or mine, but we're happy in those moments, in our little song together.

Mr Mathias pulls up a chair and sits in front of me instead of behind his big imposing teak desk. He guides me gently, so I'm standing between his knees, and his ears sink down slightly, taking his glasses with them, as he breaks into a big, friendly smile. Mr Mathias has jet-black hair which is combed straight back from his forehead. His thin-rimmed spectacles sit on the end of his big bulbous nose. But it's his big bushy eyebrows that fascinate me; I can hardly drag my eyes away from them to his lips as they dance like two furry black caterpillars as he begins to talk. He's telling me he's going to take a mould for my hearing aids today. He looks happy too and his bushy eyebrows fly up and down as he explains how he's going to do it. He shows me the tub he's going to scoop gooey putty from.

I sit down on the chair while he gets up to get the rest of his equipment. Mam smiles enthusiastically from her chair, chatting occasionally to Mr Mathias as he goes about preparing the putty. He mixes it with a little red dye, then carefully scoops the putty into a big fat plastic syringe. He looks like he's about to ice a gigantic cake.

Then, very gently, he moves my hair back and slowly and precisely pushes the putty out of the syringe and around the top of my ear.

The warm mixture tickles as it oozes into every tiny crease, and I giggle and squirm.

Mam taps my knee so I look at her to lip-read. 'Keep very still for Mr Mathias,' she tells me.

A minute later and he's done the other ear. 'There you are,' he says, handing me the leftover putty he's squirted out of the syringe. 'You better be quick before it goes hard.' The moulds he's made for me are already hardening in his big hands. I squidge the spare putty between my fingers and into my fist and giggle as it fits tightly into my palm. I show Mam and she smiles and nods. As we skip out of Mr Mathias's office and along the corridor, my squidgy ball is fast-hardening in my hands. I look at Mam as she tells me we'll be back in a couple of weeks to get my hearing aids fitted. I smile back at her, nodding.

My silent world is all I've ever known. I don't understand as yet why I'd need anything else but this quiet, or what difference Mr Mathias will make to my life. But for Mam the hearing aids can't come quick enough – especially after what happened in Blackpool.

It didn't seem like a bad thing to me, but I've seen the worry on her face when she tells her friends the story. We went there for the day a few weeks ago. We'd gone on the bus. Mam had packed spam sandwiches, and dressed me and Julie in matching striped T-shirts, shorts, knee-high white socks and sandals. 'Joanne wants a drink,' Julie would tell Mam from our bus seats, and Mam would reach into her cool bag to get us a pop. The tiny windows at the top of the bus were open and made our bunches sway in the breeze as we sped along the road to the seaside. It was a lovely hot day, we had donkey rides on the beach and then Mam wanted to look around the shops. I stared at the sticks of rock in shop windows as hordes of people brushed past me in my pushchair. I wanted to walk too. I was too hot. I wanted to go back to the donkeys on the beach. I wanted to swim in the sea. I wanted a drink. So while Mam was busy looking in a shop window, I wriggled in my pushchair, managing to get the straps loose from my shoulders first, and next the clasp that held me in. And then . . . freedom.

The next time Mam looked down, I was gone.

I knew how panicked she must have been by the way she told her friends what happened back home in our kitchen. She put her head in her hands as she told Auntie Edna; I think she was crying.

She'd searched for me everywhere, but knew there was no point in calling my name in the crowds – how would a deaf girl ever have heard? Mam was frantic. Two whole hours went by. And then finally, as the crowd parted, she saw a policeman wearing his helmet, and me tucked into the crook of his arm, grinning away quite happily. She grabbed me and wrapped me up in a hug, crying and kissing me the whole time.

The best bit was, I got an ice cream. But for Mam there was never more reason to get me these hearing aids.

I'm back in the children's hospital and sitting at a table. In front of me are some marbles. I remember them from before. My eyes scan for the yellow one with the brown flecks without luck.

Mr Mathias wants me to do the same test as before. He's indicating to me that when I hear something, I need to put a marble in the jar. I nod, remembering what I did a few weeks ago. Remembering how pleased Mam had looked each time another marble fell against the glass.

But there's something different this time. I'm not wearing the heavy black headphones that weigh down on my head. Instead, I have these strange plastic things on top of my ear. They feel weird, alien. Like they're making the tops of my ears stick out.

'These are your hearing aids,' Mr Mathias had said just a few moments ago, smiling at me and holding out two mushroom-coloured bugs. Mam had seemed delighted that they fit me; she'd clasped her hands together, grinning and nodding. I'd smiled back, unsure why she was so happy. But as far as Mam was concerned, a deaf child had got the bus here with her today and a hearing one would be going home.

She'd been trying to explain to me for weeks what was going to happen. She'd point to her ears, make a switching gesture like when she turned the dial on the television, and then she'd quickly spread out her fingers by her ears and grin, eyes sparkling. Sound. That's what she was promising me. These hearing aids will unmute the world to me; they'll turn up the volume. Just like on the television, Mam had told me back home.

But as I sit waiting for them to start the test, nothing feels any different. I can't hear Mam or Mr Mathias. I see their lips move, but the movement isn't accompanied by words. Instead a strange white noise rattles around my head. Perhaps to you it's like putting your head underwater at the swimming pool, a muffled blur of dull noise. Yes, something rather than the silence that has been my constant companion. But not sound.

'OK?' Mr Mathias is nodding. They're about to start the test.

Mam clasps her hands tighter; I know she's willing me on. But as the test starts, as Mam hears the noises, the marbles stay on the table. Or most of them, anyway. She can't hide the disappointment in her eyes, though she does her best.

There's a slight improvement, Mr Mathias tells her afterwards. They can try adjusting them. We'll see how we get on for the next few weeks, he says.

And the next thing I know, Mam is reaching for my hand. I leave hospital with these strange things behind my ears.

As we step out into the sunshine, a bus goes by. There's a strange whooshing sound in my ears, which I've never experienced before. I reach up to touch my hearing aids, then look up at Mam.

'You'll get used to them, Joanne,' she says, cocking her head to one side.

But no sound accompanies the words that leave her mouth. I'm still lip-reading.

As Mam places me in the minibus, I do everything I can to resist her. I kick, I buck, I scream, I try to cling onto her, but she gently – yet firmly – unpeels my fingers from her clothes, and puts me into the seat regardless.

I can see the pain etched on her face; I know that sending me away each day is breaking her heart. I might *see* that she's trying to reason with me, I can see her lips moving, but of course I can't hear the reassuring words she's trying to calm me with. All I know is that I don't want to go to the deaf school in this taxi, I don't want to leave Mam and Julie. Through my tears I can see a blurry image of her standing on the doorstep watching the usual morning chaos unfold.

I'm two and a half now and every day for the last few weeks I've been collected for school by this taxi. I cry every single morning as soon as the car pulls up outside the front of the house and I see her cross the room to fetch my coat and bag. I'm too young to be sent off to nursery school all day.

Or at least that was Mam's instinct when Mr Mathias first suggested I attend.

But as a deaf child, these are the adjustments I have to make now. I have to be independent because this school is good for me. It will teach me to speak, Mam tells me. *But I don't want to speak*, I think, as the taxi pulls away and the tears sting my eyes. *I want to stay at home with Mam.*

My sobs don't abate until we reach the school twenty minutes later. The part of town in which Lindisfarne School is situated is a far cry from the neat tree-lined street and the rolling countryside where our home is. The council estate that wraps around the building is situated just under the flyover that provides a link between Gateshead and Newcastle. The nearby views are of an industrial estate rather than the lush green fields around our home. Tower blocks shoot up from the ground like imposing concrete trees. Hearing children pour out of them every morning to enter this ugly prefabricated school. Their ties are skewed, their hair barely brushed, the remains of breakfast – the odd toast crumb or margarine – still clinging to their cheeks. Their grubby school blouses, desperate for a wash, waft untucked in places from their waistbands.

I'm lifted gently from the taxi, my hair in two neat bunches and tied with ribbons. My brown pinafore dress with its sweet floral trim is pressed and clean. I wear knee-high socks and T-bar Clarks shoes.

Lindisfarne is on a different side of town, there's no doubt, but the warmth of the community there more than makes up for the fact that the residents might not be bringing home the same pay-slips as the dads up on our estate.

The deaf unit is part of the ordinary primary school and is the only one in the area. Hearing and deaf children alike pile through the school gates each morning. Some on my minibus have come from miles around for a chance to learn how to communicate. It might not be the place that every parent would wish to send their child to school, but every single one of our mams and dads is grateful for the chance that we're here.

As I'm led across the car park towards the single-storey school building, I feel a soft, warm hand fit into mine. It's my friend Gillian from our estate. Our mams have been friends since we were born; her elder sister Alison is friends with our Julie. And, by sheer coincidence, she had been diagnosed as deaf around the same time as me.

By now I've sniffed all my tears away. Mam hates to see me cry every morning; I can see it breaks her heart. She's tried everything to soothe me, even getting in and riding along, then walking back with Julie.

But nothing works. I only start crying again when I have to go into class. So instead she has no choice but to let me go alone. All she can do is assure herself it's for the best.

23

As we cross the school assembly hall with its brown geometric print wallpaper, we enter our little classroom. It's a cosy room with a low ceiling and big windows; its blue walls are decorated with colourful letters and pictures. The whole of the alphabet snakes its way around the room, wrapping us in those vowels and consonants we're here to learn.

There's a standing black-and-white television at one end of the room and a rug for us all to sit down on. Our teacher, Mrs Jackson, opens up her arms wide to welcome us every morning. Her warmth means I never need miss Mam once I'm here.

'Hello, my children,' she says to us.

The seven of us sit cross-legged on the carpet in front of her and our day begins. Any other nursery school might find it hard to get – and keep – the attention of seven toddlers, but deaf children concentrate perhaps that little bit harder than hearing children. All eyes are on the teacher, lip-reading as she starts the class. The three boys have a condition called microtia, or little ears, where the outer ears haven't developed.

Under each letter of the alphabet on the wall is a basket filled with toys that begin with that letter.

Mrs Jackson puts the 'B' basket in the middle of the rug. It's jam-packed with balls, Barbies, bats, babies, binoculars. Each of us scrabble to the basket and pick something out. Then Mrs Jackson hands us all a balloon and a feather. These two seemingly meaningless objects are a vital part of how we learn to speak. As we each say the name of the toy we're playing with, Mrs Jackson encourages us to put the balloon to our lips, to feel the vibration as we say it.

'Ball,' she says into the latex balloon. We all copy. I pick up my red balloon and put it to my nose and lips. 'Baaaa,' I try to copy. I giggle as the vibrations go through the balloon and tickle my nose. Mrs Jackson moves her balloon away from her face and taps me on the knee, so I watch her say it again.

'Ba*ll*,' she says, so I can see her tongue flick forward in her mouth towards her lips as she emphasises the 'l', then she indicates to me to put the red balloon back in front of my mouth.

I try again.

'Baaa . . .' I feel my wet tongue lick my lips. I feel like I'm doing the right thing, but I'm not to know that it doesn't sound right.

Mrs Jackson tries again. Her patience knows no bounds with us.

The feather is for words with a soft sound in them, like 'babies'. We first try it with the balloon to get the 'b's. '*Ba*B*ies.*' Then quickly put the feather to our lips so we can feel the soft vibrations of each individual tuft. The feathers tickle our lips and make us giggle. Gillian and I roll on the floor, a balloon in one hand, a feather in another, before sitting back up and trying another word.

'*Bat.*' We try picking up the balloon again. We feel the way it vibrates to the 't', telling us it's a hard sound. *Bbbbatttt*! We practise for hours and hours each day as we play. Going over the same words, getting to grips with the same consonants and vowels. Mrs Jackson manages to make it feel like fun, even when we must have attempted the word 'ball' fifty or more times.

Then we go home, and try again the next day. Day after day we go around the alphabet frieze – all so that, one day, we can be part of the hearing world.

Julie is seven years old now, I am four, and she is my world. If she has her blonde hair down, I want my hair down. If she has ribbons tied in, I want them too. Mam often buys us the same clothes; I like it when she puts us in matching T-shirts – Julie has a green stripey one, I have yellow – or matching dresses.

One day I'm going to be big like Julie. I can watch her for hours as she darts around the living room, up and down our brown furry sofa, dancing and singing. That's what she's always doing. I might not know all the words or even the tune that leaves her mouth, but I love watching her all the same.

Julie loves anything musical. She puts on plays in our back garden, roping in all the kids from up and down the street. The McCormacks, the Rankin boys, Richard and Michael, who live next door. And the Canessas who live exactly opposite. Lois is a couple of years older than me, Jonathan and Stephen are her brothers. It doesn't matter to Lois that I'm not in their hearing world; she never once leaves me out. She dresses me up from the huge box of clothes we keep in the wash house, and leads me to my grassy places on her 'stage' to no doubt perform 'The Sound of Music'.

She'll make sure I'm looking at her before she explains exactly what I need to do. These days she knows she needs to tap me so I turn my head towards her before she starts talking. It's become second nature to her since I was diagnosed deaf.

I'm blissfully unaware of the amount of times that Julie has had to remind one of our friends that I can't hear. Or tell strangers in the street who call out at me to get out of the way in the supermarket. She's very protective of me. She still instinctively knows what I need, usually before I do. She tells Mam when I want a drink, when I'm hungry. She's been speaking for me well before anyone knew that my world was a silent one.

And, just like Mam, she can be my ears too. I know when the ice-cream man has arrived in our street not because I hear the little tune ringing through our back door, but because Julie jumps up from the sofa and dashes off to get some pennies from Mam's purse.

I run after her, then watch from the gate as she brings back two Lemonade Sparkles from the ice-cream van. She has a big grin on her face, and couldn't look more pleased with herself if she was bringing home the FA Cup for Newcastle United. But she's four years older than me, and there are things that she can do, and I can't.

At seven, she can ask Mam to go out to play in the street with her friends. There's a church of the Latter-day Saints at the top of our street and everyone plays there in the car park when it's empty.

I watch from the gate, scanning the pathway for any sign of her return. I've escaped a couple of times too, so desperate am I to play with the bigger kids.

Even to me in my already silent world, the house is quiet without Julie. Mam tries to keep me amused as she peels potatoes from a giant brown sack to make chips for tea, but I just stand by the gate, waiting to catch a glimpse of Julie's blonde hair peeping over the hydrangeas in our front garden. The best times with Julie are always snuggling up on the sofa. I link her arm and beam up at her.

But right now, Mam is cross with her. We're in the living room, me on the brown sofa and Julie stamping her feet on the rug in the middle.

'I can't hear the television,' she's wailing to Mam. Her face is red and cross. 'It's not loud enough.'

Mam turns it up, but still she goes on. 'Turn it up more,' she cries. 'I can't hear.'

I look at the screen. I stare at the pictures while Julie carries on complaining to Mam.

Finally, Mam loses her temper. She storms across the room and turns the dial anti-clockwise to switch the sound off altogether. 'There,' she says. 'Now you know what it's like for Joanne.' Julie looks at me and slumps down on the brown sofa, arms crossed. But she never complains that she can't hear something ever again.

Chapter Three

It is true that when one sense is diminished, another sense becomes more acute in its place. Perhaps that's why Mam says my nose is always twitching like a little rabbit's – because my sense of smell is so sensitive. Quite often I've jumped out of bed when Mam and Dad have ordered a Chinese

Freshly cut grass, turps and tar: they are the smells that mean summer to me. They are long, hot days playing out with friends, running into each other's houses to grab a drink or a Mr Freeze ice pop from the freezer, or pausing from our games to swap our skates for our bikes, a space hopper for a Rubik's cube. Our older brothers and sisters each have the latter, which looked so easy when they unwrapped them at Christmas time – neatly arranged lines of orange, green, red covering each side of the cube – but these days they're multicoloured jumbles which have defeated each of them since the day they were taken out of the box.

On hot days the tarmac bubbles in the road and we pop it with our lollipop sticks. The draw of the wet, shiny black goo is irresistible to us, despite the fact that the grown-ups tell us over and over that it's dirty and we'll get it all over our clothes. Mam's pleas to stay away from it echo up the street in Julie's ears long after we've headed to the Mormon car park at the top of our road to get up to more sticky business away from the eyes of our prying parents.

Calamine is another smell that always means school holidays to me, running in to Mam when I've fallen in a pile of nettles, or having heaps of it applied at night after hot baths with Julie that make our sunburn sting. The pink cream Mam applies offers momentary relief to our scorched shoulders until they hit the bedsheets, and we face another night of heat radiating from our red bodies. The next day we're sent out wearing T-shirts instead of vests to offer our toasted skin some respite from the sun's rays, but we just return that evening for tea with our forearms beaming, as we pick up our knives and forks and tuck into ham-and-egg pie with steaming chips fresh from the chip-pan.

At weekends we put on one of Julie's plays that we've been rehearsing all week, offering refreshments to our parents who patiently sit in garden chairs alongside the snap dragon borders. We dilute orange juice and give it a freshly mowed grass 'topper', and serve it in a range of plastic beakers that we've pilfered from each of our kitchens while our mams weren't looking.

In the summer holidays we often visit our nana in Ripon. Nana Taylor – Mary, Dad's mam – is always smiling: that's how I think of her when we're back home in Gateshead. She's always smartly dressed with pearls, and never without matching shoes and handbag. She often has a tiny glass of sherry in her hand, or she'll be knitting. She wears beautiful cat eye glasses framed by the tight curls of her shampoo and set. She loves it when we're there, family is everything to her, but then she came from a big family herself.

She was one of seven, Byker born and bred. She emigrated to New Zealand with her brother Fred when she was eighteen, but came back home because she missed Geordieland so much. That's when she met James Milne, or Granddad Shep as Julie always calls him (they had a dog called Shep, Mam says, when they laugh about Julie calling him that). He died a few months after I was born, but Nana has lots of pictures of him all around the house in Ripon.

Her house is an array of different smells to me; her dressing table with its crocheted mat and dainty tablecloths, countless delicate perfume bottles and jars of creams is a sensory treasure chest. Rose water and lavender talc vie to outdo each other in the scent stakes. And a hug from Nana is another pleasant assault on the olfactory senses: magnolia and primrose odours stay on my clothes long after her arms have uncurled themselves from me and we're on our way back home in the car – though probably no one else would realise.

I remember the day I discovered holy water on her dressing table. I carefully unscrewed the lid, convinced I was in for a real treat, but instead of smelling of God, it smelled no different to the stuff that comes out of our tap back home in Gateshead; perhaps slightly less chlorinated.

Downstairs in her little cottage, dried prunes, nuts and raisins are laid out in little dishes on her coffee table. Julie never seems to notice they are there but their fruity smell radiates out from the centre of the room as soon as I walk in, making it impossible for my eyes not to be drawn to them.

Perhaps I think that everyone smells like I do; perhaps I don't realise that in place of my ears I have been granted a different gift that colours in my world in a way that my hearing friends don't have.

Back home on the Chowdene estate, Stephen Canessa and I go up and down the streets on warm sunny days picking up the rose petals that have fallen onto the pavement, or daring each other to steal the best ones from people's gardens. We take our stash back home and stuff them into jam jars with water in the hope of making a perfume sweet enough for our mams.

But the murky juice accompanied by the floating bits of grass or the odd black insect is no match for the Old Spice that Dad wears. Weekends in our house when Dad is back from work: the air is filled with the scent of those tubby white bottles complete with famous ship motif, mixed with a hint of tobacco and the black bullet mints he keeps in his work van. And weekends also mean hugs from Dad, cuddles in his lap in front of the TV, and him chasing me and Julie and our friends round the garden as he pretends to be the Incredible Hulk.

Yet it's Mam's Estée Lauder Youth Dew that is the constant accompaniment to my childhood. This musky fragrance lingers every time she leaves the room even if, for me, her voice doesn't.

Except for the last few days, Mam's sweet odour has been missing from our house. It's no surprise to us as her belly has been growing bigger over the summer of 1979, almost as quickly as

Julie and I are stretching out of our matching sundresses. A few weeks ago, I wondered if Mam might actually go pop.

I've loved cuddling up to Mam in the last few months, feeling the new baby wriggling and squirming under my head as I give her bump a cuddle. 'That's the baby saying hello,' she'd tell me as I giggled and put my hand on her bump to catch another kick or perhaps some hiccups.

Dad is looking after us while Mam's not here. Right now we're sitting in Greggs on the Fell. Both Julie and I have a raspberryade and a sticky iced bun. I pick at the pink icing, scooping up big chunks with my index fingers and popping them into my mouth as Dad tells us about our new little sister. The goo collects under my fingernails, and I tease it out with my tongue, making the flavour linger for longer.

The new baby is called Alana and soon Dad is taking us to see her. 'She's very tiny,' he tells us as we slurp up the last of our raspberryade, the straw clearly making a big noise in the cafe because people are turning to look. Julie giggles and I laugh along with her, despite the fact that I can't hear a sound.

'Come on,' Dad says as he takes our hands and we walk up to the hospital. As we skip along beside him, trying to keep up with his great big strides, I have a funny feeling in my tummy. It's not the iced bun that's made it feel tender, instead it's a fluttery tickle, like all the bubbles from the raspberryade are jumping and dancing inside me wanting to meet the new baby too. But as we get closer to the maternity ward, I realise I'm nervous to meet her. What will she look like? How will she feel? Will she know I'm her sister? Will she like me?

I can see the Queen Elizabeth Hospital now: big high buildings that remind me of the tower blocks that surround my school. I hesitate as Dad's hand momentarily slips out of mine to open the door and lead us in. The questions in my head are still coming thick and fast: will Mam look poorly? How did they get the baby out? What will happen to her bump?

Dad is chattering away to Julie as an endless stream of questions circle round inside my head. I watch as they talk to each other, but what about I don't know because I'm not concentrating on their lips. Instead my eyes are scanning the clean, white hospital corridors, searching for Mam. The smells of disinfectant and something like school dinners mingle in my nostrils. There are people in wheelchairs, and some wandering around in dressing gowns; there are others smoking in pyjamas just outside the hospital doors. Mostly there are old people, but I spot one boy about my age: his arm is in plaster and he looks sad. Does it hurt, I wonder to myself. Will Mam be wearing a plaster cast, or perhaps the baby will?

Dad leads us down one long corridor after another, as I try to keep up with his long stride. Dad knows where he's going, he leads us this way and that while I wonder if this is where he came when Mam had me from her belly.

And then finally we're here. My heart skips a beat as Dad opens the doors to the ward and I see rows and rows of ladies in bed wearing white nighties. Their babies are proudly displayed in plastic incubators beside them while nurses in crisply pressed blue uniforms buzz about. Here there's a lighter scent mixed in with the hospital bleach, a sweet milky smell, and as we walk past bed after bed, my eyes quickly scan the incubators for a glimpse of the babies, but instead all I see is a mass of blankets, perhaps a flash of pink head.

And then among the anonymous series of ladies in beds, I see . . . *Mam!* She's sitting up in bed, wearing her familiar pink nightie from home. She's wearing the biggest smile I've ever seen, which instantly puts my five-year-old heart at rest as I race over and lean in for a hug.

Mam is OK, and there beside her is the tiniest pinkiest baby I've ever seen, all wrapped up in white blankets with only her weeny face poking out. She's sleeping away, eyes closed, perfect little button nose, and rosebud lips. So this is what was in Mam's tummy. I stare, mesmerised.

Mam taps my shoulder and I tear my eyes away from the incubator. 'This is your baby sister, Alana,' she tells me, her eyes twinkling with happiness.

I reach into the incubator and touch one of Alana's little lined hands. Her fingers instantly close around mine, and I giggle, delighted. I stand here for at least ten minutes, not wanting to let go of my little baby sister even for a second, her warm grip on my index finger never ceasing as she sleeps, and my eyes dancing with the same delight I'd seen in Mam's.

I've never felt so big and strong – and so proud of Mam – as I do right now.

Every morning Mam picks out another pretty outfit for me to wear to school. I have one favourite white T-shirt with yellow scallop-edged sleeves and with it I always wear the same lemon pleated skirt that swishes round my knees. Another pink dress is edged around the collar with a burst of colourful flowers. Mam combs my hair into two bunches and secures them with pastel-coloured ribbons. She pays equal attention to Julie. By the time we leave for school, we both look a picture.

Except that's where the similarity ends.

Because on top of my pretty dress, I need to wear my phonic ear. It's a hard metallic box about the size of a paperback book that weighs down in the middle of my tiny chest, and it is secured with thick ugly straps that dig into my shoulders. With its big round speaker in the front, it makes me look like a robot, or so I was told.

The box hooks up to my hearing aids and amplifies the little I can hear. Imagine swimming underwater: the muffled white noise that echoes in your ear, indistinguishable words but sometimes just the faint whisper of a sound, so fleeting I could miss it, or perhaps a low hum in a room that's actually alive with people, or a very gentle tap if a plate clatters to the floor. Sometimes it feels like I'm a million miles away from real noise, but what the phonic box does is give me something, the odd shape of a word, or a deep, low grumble. Without it, there is silence, and even with it I still use my eyes to listen.

The box speaks wirelessly to the microphone that Mrs Jackson wears in class, which amplifies her voice, constantly testing our ears to work a little bit harder. Sometimes I can just make out the 'b' in 'ball' when we're going through the alphabet. Or the phonic ear might offer me the 't' at the end of 'cat' as a rare treat to fill in the silence.

We were given the phonic ears once we turned four and 'proper' lessons started in our class. Instead of playing with us on the mat as toddlers, Mrs Jackson sat us behind little chairs and tables to teach us just like the other children.

We did maths and spellings and learnt how to write by copying Mrs Jackson from the blackboard, while she stood at the front, clutching the mic that speaks to our phonic ears.

But I hate wearing it more than anything because it firmly separates me from my friends on the Chowdene estate. As I climb into the taxi each morning wearing my phonic ear, I see all the other children in my street leaving for school without a giant bulge under their winter coats, and I don't want to be different. I don't *see* myself as different, so why do I have to wear something that tells the whole world I am?

The children at Lindisfarne Infants School are used to us deaf children and our strange phonic boxes. They don't need to ask questions; they know that it is there to help us hear.

I remember when I first got it there was just one child in the playground – perhaps he was new to the school – who asked me what it was.

'I'm deaf,' I said, as he poked at it. 'It helps me to hear.'

He tipped his head to one side. 'Aww,' he said, turning his mouth down at the edges.

'It's OK,' I said. 'It doesn't hurt.'

But it does make me stand out from the crowd. I long for home time when I can rip it off my shoulders, but these days even then I don't get any respite. Mam is delighted that my teachers have allowed her to keep a microphone at home.

'Aren't we lucky, Joanne?' she mouths to me.

So each day after school she sits at the kitchen table with me speaking into the mic and making me practise my words all over again. But I don't feel lucky at all.

I watch Julie running in and out of the house without a care in the world, coming back and forth with her friends for a drink, a skipping rope, their bikes, and I envy them their freedom. Why can't I come home and play outside like Julie? If I didn't have to wear this box, I could. If I wasn't deaf, I could.

Mam's patience knows no bounds though. She has three of us girls to care for now, but as Alana sits and gurgles in her highchair chewing on a rusk, and dinner bubbles away on the stove, Mam will repeat word after word into the microphone as a trickle of shapes and sounds filter through my ears, and her voice tires from talking.

I hate the fact that this phonic ear is marking me out as different, but each day Mam feels that it's doing a little bit more to make me the same.

The ground feels hard and cold underneath me and a few sharp pebbles dig into my scalp. I scrape my fingers along the tarmac and feel grit collecting under my nails. I can see the tops of my red T-bar shoes if I look down, but mostly I can just see sky – lots of it – as I lie flat on my back. It's an overcast day so there's not a glimpse of blue between the clouds, just one big blanket of grey fluff that fills up the sky above me, melting into my eyes and flowing into my ears. I guess sometimes it feels as if my ears were stuffed full of some similar soft cloud-like substance; as if that's the thing that mutes everything for me, soaking up the sound I should be hearing.

Wouldn't it be nice to just pull it out, like you do a folded ream of cotton wool from a bag, heave from one end until sound flooded into my eardrum for the first time? I'd be able to hear my friends as they called me up and down our street; I'd actually know when it's time to run indoors for Mam's purse because *I* can hear the ice-cream van, or the sound of Mam's voice calling us in for tea. I'd be able to watch the TV like Julie, listening to the words instead of just watching the pictures.

And then of course there are the sounds I might not like: Mam scolding us for covering our clothes in mud or getting grass stains on our white shorts, or the piercing sound of Alana's cries. When my little baby sister is crying because she's hungry, would I sit like Julie does on the sofa, covering her ears, or would I sit and smile and let it flow through me because I'm just so grateful to hear anything at all?

It might be a moment like this one now. I wouldn't like to hear the fear in Mam's voice as she comes running out of the front door to find me lying in the road, the car that hit me stopped just feet away.

I can't hear the relief in her voice when she finds me unhurt, just like I didn't hear the roar of the driver's engine or the screech of his brakes as I stepped off the path. My eyes had forgotten just for a second to search the road for the tell-tale flash of metal paintwork before we headed out for the afternoon. Instead, I just felt the side of the car as it clipped me, knocking me down in the street as Mam struggled out of the house with Alana in her pram.

'Joanne, are you hurt?' Mam is kneeling on the tarmac beside me, her eyes quickly scanning my body for signs of blood, and her shoulders relaxing as she fails to find any. But my phonic box is squashed flat where I landed.

'It's OK,' I say, taking one last glimpse at the clouds before I get up and wipe the grit from my clothes. 'I'm not dead.'

Mam heaves a sigh of relief, then takes me by the shoulders and tells me I *must* be more careful. She's firm, but the love and relief is still twinkling in her eyes as she pulls me close. The driver of the car was more shaken up. He gives me a shiny 50p piece to say sorry.

I notice an elderly lady has stopped on the other side of the road with her fabric shopping trolley to take a good look at the drama as the driver gets back into his car. She shakes her head and I know Mam tries not to notice. But sometimes it's impossible not to. People on this estate know I'm the Deaf Girl: they wonder why Mam lets me play out in the street with my friends at all; they don't think it's safe for me to play outside.

And sometimes, I can see, Mam doesn't think so either. But what's the alternative? To have me sitting in all day, to never climb trees or learn to ride a bike, to play inside with jigsaws instead of risking falling and grazing my knee? I know Mam doesn't think that's any life for me, or any child: it would be like caging a bird.

Yet I can see for myself that her heart is pounding with fear each time she picks me up after a fall: could she – *should* she – have prevented this? She asks herself the same question every day.

This isn't the first time I've been knocked down by a car. She had the same look the last time I was knocked over, or when I came off my bike a few weeks ago. Did I fall off because I'm deaf, or because I'm a child? She tells herself it's the latter. In spite of her fears, Mam has always insisted that my deafness should not prevent me from doing anything. 'There is nothing that you can't do,' she tells me. And she means it. We just have to find a different way to do it.

We don't need to learn to sign at home. Mam, Dad, Julie or Granddad just remember to tap my shoulder or get my attention before they start to speak to me, so I can lip-read. If Julie wants me from the other side of the room when we're all playing, she asks one of her friends to tap me, or marches over and stands right in front of me.

Mam doesn't turn towards the cooker and chat like others would: she makes a point of us talking round the table while we have dinner each night. And, just like Mr Mathias, Granddad pulls me between his knees when he's asking me about my day at school, so I can clearly see his lips as he questions me. These are tiny things that make me feel *enabled* rather than disabled. I never feel any different from Julie at home. I never have because everyone adapts. It's second nature to them now.

I'm almost seven now, and I have reached the end of my time at Lindisfarne. There will be no more taxi to school, now it's time to move up to juniors. Most of my deaf friends are going to a boarding school miles away – Gillian is going too. I'm afraid that I won't see her again, but Mam promises me she'll be home in the school holidays. At the deaf school, everything is geared towards being deaf – they'll learn sign language instead of lip-reading – but Mam refuses to send me there. She wants me to go to the same school as Julie.

Mam and Granddad have been disappearing for meeting after meeting at the school. I don't need to lip-read to be able to understand that some of the teachers don't want a deaf child there. Mam has been telling them that I don't need special attention, I just need them to turn to the front to address the class; I just need to be able to see their lips. But they're not keen.

Sometimes Mam takes me along to speak to the headteacher when she's picking up Julie. You don't need ears to hear the resistance to her pleas for me to start at Oakfield Juniors, their body language speaks a thousand silent words. I've got used to reading the little signals that other people might miss: the folded arms, the hands gesticulating, the pursed lips or hard set eyes.

But Mam isn't put off, she keeps on. She is a strong Geordie woman, after all, and like the women in her family before her, she won't take no for an answer. It doesn't matter that she's on her own for most of the week, she won't accept any less than what she believes her daughter deserves. She's a mam, and all she wants is what's best for her children – all three of us.

I've seen the toll this fight has taken on her, though. I can see the frustration in her eyes, and feel the tension as she grips my hand and leads me away from yet another unsuccessful meeting with the school. They don't want to change their teaching methods to include a deaf student. Why should thirty children in a class have to compromise for me, they wonder. But Mam – backed up by our social worker Mrs McLellan – insists they wouldn't need to, that it's about including me, that all they need to do is let me see their faces when they speak, let me lip-read. She makes it sound easy, she insists it is, despite the blank stares that infuriate her, or one teacher's unkind suggestion that maybe they should paint their lips white to help me see better.

But I know something the school don't: she won't give up.

So they better had.

Chapter Four

I've practised all week for this, and now it's here: our weekly spelling test. I sit at the front of the class, my pencil hovering above the faint line in anticipation and my eyes fixed on my teacher. I can't bear to look away even for a second to sharpen my pencil in case the test starts and I miss the first word. So while my friends chatter amongst themselves, sure not to miss the teacher's voice when she starts talking, my eyes follow her round the room, and my tummy twists a little in nervous expectancy.

Mam has been so patient with me all week, going through the spellings in my narrow grey book over and over again. One hand holding the mic that speaks to my phonic ear, and the other stirring dinner or jostling Alana in her lap. There are twenty words to spell in total, and I've spent the last few days getting them down perfectly. After reading them out each evening, Mam would lean over and check how many I'd managed, then give me a pat on the shoulder as her face broke into a smile: 'Well done, Joanne!'

And now, as I sit here waiting for the test to start, I can't wait for my teacher to see how much work I've put in too. All week I've been picturing how proud she'll be of me when she sees me get twenty out of twenty.

And now, here it is. She picks up her book, clears her throat and starts to read from the list.

'Manager.'

I see my teacher mouth the word, and I'm off, frantically scribbling down the letters I've become so familiar with all week. *M. . .A. . .N. . .A. . .G. . .E. . .R.*

I know it's right the minute I see it down on paper. I swell briefly with pride, before I look up to catch the next word. I have to be quick, writing a bit quicker than my friends, so there's no chance of missing the next word.

L. . .A. . .M. . .P. . .S. . .H. . .A. . .D. . .E. My head flies down again and the lead of my pencil scratches against the paper. I look up, ready for the next word – but what's this? She's turning away from me. I panic. *No, turn back.* I see the other children's heads go down, watch as they start scribbling furiously with their pencils, but I have no idea what she's said.

Stop, slow down, I think.

But before I have a chance to put my hand up, I see my classmates' heads fly down again, the concentration as they write one word after another. The next, the next, the next, and all the time the teacher is staring out of the window as she reads instead of looking out at the class so I can lip-read.

45

Tears prick at my eyes and disappointment swells in my stomach as I let my pencil fall to the desk. I realise I've practised all week for nothing. I look at the first two words – the only two words – in my spelling book and wonder how I'll tell Mam what happened.

The class has finished now, the pupils all chattering happily around me, their lips working nineteen to the dozen, so relieved the test is over for another week. And as we hand our books in to be marked, my teacher doesn't notice the tears that are rolling down my cheeks and wobbling precariously on my chin, before they drop down and pool on my wooden desk. The bell goes to signal the end of the school day, I realise this must be the case because the other children push back from the desk and run out to the corridor for their coats. I shuffle behind them. This wasn't how I imagined Oakfield Junior School to be.

Mam had battled furiously to get me in and I'd been so excited all summer. I'd played out with my friends in the street, asking them what it would be like. I was used to my tiny class of six at Lindisfarne so I had no idea what it would be like to be part of a big class. I'd pictured making friends with new children, working hard to make the teachers proud, and running round at playtime with all my friends from the Chowdene estate.

When September rolled round and the green leaves on the trees started to fade to orange and yellow, I was thrilled to be able to walk into school with my friends instead of getting into a taxi that would shuttle me across town and away from everyone and everything that was so familiar. This is what I'd dreamt of for years – to be just like the rest of the children on my street.

And yet I've quickly come to realise – even at my young age – that people tend to fall into two categories in life: the ones who want to help you, and the ones who want to help themselves. Despite Mam's pleas that the teachers didn't need to change the way they taught because they had a deaf girl in the class, that they just needed to make sure I could see their faces to lip-read, half of the teachers didn't see why they had to make any changes at all. If they wanted to go over and look out of the window – like my teacher had today – then so they should. Some even moaned about the fact that Mam had requested I always sit at the front of the class.

I'd given up putting my hand up and asking the teacher to repeat the spelling test for me; I didn't need ears to be able to hear their exasperated sighs. Some teachers had little patience and mistook my confidence to point out that they'd turned away as insolence. They'd throw chalk at me if I started chatting to a friend, not realising that they'd started a lesson whilst writing on the blackboard as they spoke.

I still remember the first time I was sent to 'The Bridge'. That was where the naughty children had to stand, on a glass walkway outside the headmaster's office. I sobbed and sobbed the first time I was sent there. I'd been thrown out of the class for talking, but I wasn't to know at the time that the teacher was talking too.

We were made to stand in front of huge pillars and each of them was decorated with giant maps of the world. They were so colourful – pinks and greens, purples and yellows – and in 3D too, so that when you touched a mountainous country you felt the bumps under your fingers. The other kids joked that if you were on The Bridge you must be good at geography because there was nothing else to do there but stare at these maps and learn the fifty-one states of America, or which countries made up the USSR.

At first I felt so ashamed standing there, but it became such a regular occurrence that, in time, I'd often just shrug as I was sent for another detention; the start of me developing my thick skin, perhaps.

As time went on, I'd giggle on The Bridge as I got to know some of the naughtiest boys in the school. We'd swap places when the headmaster wasn't watching, then chortle as he looked up confused because we weren't standing at the same pillar anymore.

Around the dining table at home, Mam would encourage us to talk about our day. Whenever I told her I'd been on The Bridge again, she'd put down her knife and fork, disappointed. 'What was it this time?' she'd ask.

And I'd tell her I got caught sharpening my pencil when the teacher was trying to demonstrate something.

She didn't excuse what I did but always looked for solutions. 'Have you thought about keeping two sharp pencils in your case, Joanne?' she'd suggest. 'That way you'd always have one ready.'

She always thought there might be something else I could do to save it happening again.

But a week later – despite the two newly sharpened HBs in my fluffy pencil case – I'd be back on The Bridge again, this time for something else. Mam would march down to the school, ploughing on, always polite but reminding the teachers that I just needed to see their faces, and always giving my hand a little squeeze to let me know she was fighting my corner, even if I couldn't keep up with the adults talking above me.

At home, though, I'd walk in on whispered conversations between Mam and Granddad in the kitchen. They'd stop talking as I wandered in, looking for an orange Club or a mint Viscount biscuit, but if I'd been able to eavesdrop from outside, I might have heard Mam asking Granddad if she'd done the right thing at all by sending me to the school.

Yet our family motto was always to make the best of things and get on with it. Granddad would gently reassure her whenever she got worried that she was doing the right thing. He'd keep on talking until her worry lines were wiped away, a smile appearing in their place.

'Yes,' she'd say, turning back to his mince and potatoes. 'She'll be fine.'

But it wasn't just the teachers who were opposed to me being there, mostly it was the parents of other children. 'My mam says you shouldn't be at our school' came the insults across the playground, from mouths too young to know how spiteful they sounded. On days like those I would run home from school and cry to Mam and Granddad at the dinner table. 'Why don't they want me there? What's wrong with me?' I would sob.

They would tell me straight. 'Some people are cruel,' Mam would say. 'Don't take any notice.'

So on those days when other children call me a 'robot' for wearing my phonic ear at playtime, or – even worse – 'spastic' because I don't speak quite as clearly as them, I try to remember not to let it get to me. Granddad tells me stories from the wars he fought in to cheer me up. 'A man can be strong and fight in wars,' he says, 'but it's what's in his heart that really counts.' Then he puts his hand to his chest and I know what he's telling me: these children with their spiteful words and callous names shouldn't matter at all, because it's what's inside that matters. But at seven, it is sometimes hard to keep reminding myself of that.

One good thing is that, due to my deafness, I don't hear most of the insults that are thrown my way. Instead of noticing the cruel words or miming behind my back, I'm usually focused on the friends I've linked arms with so I can lip-read, the happy faces who want to talk to me. I'm not aware of just how much badness in people is passing me by. My ears and distracted eyes often save me from the greatest hurt.

But it's the ignorance shown by the teachers that hurts the worst. Because even at seven, as I walk home from school now after failing the spelling test, angrily kicking stones in my path, I know that they – more than anyone – should know better.

As 'Making Your Mind Up' by Bucks Fizz rings out across the room, all us children run around giggling. The girls skip, the boys often attempt a skid, until suddenly without warning everyone stands stock still in the same position.

There's always one child whose leg wobbles before it gives way, or someone who doesn't stop in time with the song as we race around playing musical statues at a birthday party – but that person is rarely me. Finally the music rings out again, and we all start dancing round like loonies.

You might wonder how a deaf girl can play something like

musical statues, but in our house there was always a way around everything. You see, while the other kids jump and skip around the room, they might not notice that I always keep one eye on Mam. That as I sashay from foot to foot, sweeping the floor with my toes and clicking my heels together, I'm desperately following Mam's lead, checking to see when her fingers reach for the volume dial, or the secret nod she gives me like a precious gift between two allies letting me know, any second now, the music is about to be cut. And then, like everyone else, I stand stock still, one knee trembling under the weight of my body if I've been caught, literally, on the hop.

Who knows if I'm really doing it exactly in time with the music? I always feel like I am, but just as often as everyone else I'm expelled from the dance floor, and instead watch the rest of them play from our brown furry sofa. But that's the thing about my family home: I'm never made to feel like there's anything I can't join in with.

Even at weekends, when Dad's home and we sit down to watch a film on the video player, no one will let me miss out. Every so often they'll pause the screen, making sure to fill me in on what's happening or to check that I haven't missed any part of the storyline. They never get tired of me asking: 'What did he say to her? What did she say?'

I might be deaf but, in their eyes, there's no reason why I can't enjoy a film with my family.

That's why Mam – and all of my family and friends – are my ears for me. At home I never feel like the Deaf Girl; at school, especially now Julie had left to go up to junior high, cruel children always remind me that I am.

I've been at Oakfield Junior School for a year now, and I hate it. The teachers might have adapted to my special needs, but the children won't let me forget them. The cruel names that I often can't hear have long since been replaced with punches and kicks. There is one ringleader who, like some miniature evil dictator in long white socks and bunches, casts an evil spell over the other girls in my class.

They carry out her vicious attacks for fear of her making them the next target. So I take the pinches, the punches, even the kicks, because I know the girls who deliver them live in fear as much as I do.

But, unlike the others who might have done something no more problematic than putting on the wrong dress that morning, there is always a reason to bully me: I am deaf, I am different. Do I really deserve to get a smack in the head, or a chunk of hair ripped out of my scalp, simply because I've been born without the gift of sound? Obviously they think so.

My best friend at Oakfield is Victoria. We instantly gravitated towards each other when I'd started there. We walk around the playground holding hands, me with my blonde hair, her brunette, me keeping her close so I can lip-read as we stroll over to play hopscotch.

She saw past my deafness; she never makes me feel like I am different. But sometimes it's impossible for her to disguise the hurt in her eyes when she hears someone call me a cruel name.

We keep our out-of-school friendship secret for fear of being scolded for it by the bully come Monday at school. We spend every weekend together, skipping in and out of each other's houses for a glass of pop, or at Victoria's aunty's caravan in Berwick.

I've never had a best friend before, and Victoria and I mean everything to each other. But even she is drawn into the bully's web from time to time. Among the throng that beat me up in the toilets after school, I sometimes spot a familiar face I love.

But as Victoria softly pulls my hair, instructed by the bully, she's always sure to mouth to me, 'I'm your friend really.' At the weekends we talk about it; she'll say she's sorry. And I know how it works: it's self-preservation; if she doesn't do what the bully says, it'll only happen to her too. And often it did.

The look of sadness in her eyes as she hits me doesn't stop the hurt and humiliation though. I sob all the way home, my phonic ear hanging desolately from my arms. Mam wipes away my tears and sometimes a bit of blood while I ask her over and over if my hearing aids have been damaged. I hate that phonic ear, and yet I can't bear to be without it. One wrong punch from a bully could plunge me into the silence that I so dread, away from the comfort of the white noise. Even the muffled sound of taunts, which I recognise only because they are accompanied by screwed-up faces and angry eyes, are company to my ears.

Because that silence is what I live with at night. When it's time to climb into my bunk bed in the room I share with Alana, I take out my hearing aids and leave my phonic box on the table beside our beds. If Alana and I want to gossip, we write notes on our hands. Often, I'll be lying in the dusky light and spot a pink hand waving in front of me, a smiley face scrawled on the palm in biro.

Unlike most children, I don't go to sleep to the sound of Mam pottering around in the kitchen washing dishes. Instead, the darkness and silence wash over me like a great big wave on Blackpool beach, taking me into my dreams and away from my wonderful family, but to a place where I finally have some respite from the bullies at school.

As I sit out the rest of musical statues on the sofa, I realise again how lucky my friends are to be able to run around to music.

Slowly, carefully, and with great precision, Granddad lines up the shiny five-pence pieces. I watch, my eyes as round as the coins themselves. There they are, big silver discs, all gleaming with the promise of the strawberry shoelaces or sherbet saucers I'll buy with them later.

Granddad sits behind them, his big round face smiling, the gatekeeper of this reward. He is how he always is: reliable, consistent, calm and caring. He never lets us down, and has untold patience for me and my sisters.

This is our routine now. As soon as I come through the door from school and spot his familiar hat and gloves on the dining table, I know he's here. I can smell the Imperial Leather or the scent of Brasso that lingers in the air after he's spent the afternoon polishing Mam's brassware. He goes over it with a cloth until it shines like a mirror. Then he'll move onto our school shoes once we arrive home.

We take up our positions: Granddad in a chair, me sitting cross-legged on the carpet in front of him. The only things between us are these six five-pence pieces.

I wait for his lips to start moving. 'Right, let's go through it again,' he says, putting his hands on his knees and leaning forward slightly. 'Which words did you learn today at school?'

It doesn't matter how long we're sitting there – some days it might be ten minutes, another day an hour – he has a way of making me feel that there is nothing else in the world that is more important than me at this moment. That all the clocks could stop for all he cared; the world could wait.

'Now,' he says. 'Li-bra-ry . . .'

I watch mesmerised as he mouths every syllable to me. Over and over until his jaw must surely ache, but he wants me to get it just right.

I copy what I've watched him do, and out must come the word, even though I don't hear it myself, because his face creases into a smile and he slides one of those precious five-pence pieces towards me. I do a little skip inside.

'Now,' he says. 'Which one is next?'

Granddad is devoted to us; you can tell simply from the way he looks at us. He has four grandchildren in total, us three girls and then our cousin, Andrew. Granddad is brilliant at maths and will spend hours playing Yahtzee with Andrew. He keeps a picture of himself and the four of us in pride of place at his house. But I know he and I have an extra-special bond.

Every Thursday Mam will take us girls to the Chinese restaurant in town, Blue Sky. Granddad will always be there waiting for us, waving from our familiar round table. His eyes will light up when we bound over, covering him in kisses and cuddles and vying for who can sit next to him. He's full of smiles as he listens in turn to our stories from school that week, and he's always laughing – a great, deep belly laugh, and one of the only muffled 'sounds' I can pick up with my phonic ear.

I've never heard his voice, of course, but I've often imagined what he might sound like. To me, it would be the voice of a perfect English gentleman, the type I've seen in films who always holds doors open for ladies and says his 'please' and 'thank yous. I can already tell from lip-reading that he speaks very well, pronouncing all his words perfectly, just like my speech therapist, so, for me, he is the best person to practise with. And unlike when Mam keeps me in after school to go over and over the same words while Julie skips around outside, I never mind when it's Granddad.

His military training is always there in the background: a strict look if he spots our elbows on the table at dinner; an unspoken set of rules that makes us feel safe and secure around him. But these days he's getting naughtier. He'll bang on the table at the Chinese and say, 'We want pud!' and all us children will laugh and copy him.

That's why I know he loves us so much, because he's always laughing when we're around; that lovely, deep belly laugh. One of my favourite sounds.

I open up the top of my wooden desk and already my ten-year-old heart is breaking. There they are, dumped in the hole where once an inkwell would have been. Each tiny wooden castanet is splintered and smashed, the smooth edges replaced with sharp jagged ones that look like little daggers, the anger in them apparent and the message from their senders received loud and clear.

They lie shattered in a heap, these little keyrings that I'd taken such care to pick out while on holiday in Spain a few weeks before. Mam had begged me not to buy them, she didn't see the point in spending my pocket money on them – probably because she knew that they'd end up like this. But I'd ignored her advice, and instead had spent ages picking them out, deciding between each little motif painted on the front before settling on an image of a flamenco dancer with flowing black hair. I counted up how many I'd need for each of the recipients of this holiday souvenir, then fished into my shoulder bag for my pesetas.

Mam had rolled her eyes as I'd held them up proudly. 'Joanne, are you sure you want to get them?' she'd sighed. But I'd nodded excitedly. And I'd been so enthusiastic this morning as I'd carried in my haul to school, using the same blue-and-white paper bag that the Spanish lady at the beachside shop had handed to me as she packaged up the gifts. She'd smiled at my purchases, even if Mam hadn't.

And now look at this sad little heap. My eyes are drawn to one in particular: the little flamenco lady that I'd so carefully chosen. She'd been torn in two by the sheer hatred that was used to smash up the tiny trinkets.

Today was the first day back at school after the summer break. It was my last year at Oakfield, and I was determined that this one was going to be different.

The summer holidays spent skipping around in the Spanish sunshine, jumping in and out of the pool with Alana and Julie, had seemed a million miles away from the bullies back home. My blonde hair had grown back where it had been pulled out in clumps, and the bruises had faded under the Mediterranean warmth – and so too had my hurt. And that's where I'd decided: I'd *make* these girls like me. I wouldn't have another year like the last; shuffling to the toilets after school for yet another beating, running home crying to Mam, battered and bruised, my school-books torn, my blouse ripped.

The last time it had happened, our teacher, Mr Downie, had burst in on them. I was on the floor by then, cowering from the kicks and punches. I'd spotted my phonic ear first, the straps dangling pathetically from his big hands, its owner now curled up in a ball on the cold, tiled toilet floor.

He'd shouted something at the girls and they'd all scattered. I could see in his eyes just how angry he was and, had I been wearing my phonic ear, I might have picked up a faint trace of the fury in his voice. But instead I'd used the distraction as my chance to run too. I'd grabbed my hearing aid from his arms and limped all the way home to Mam.

She was already waiting on the street as I turned the corner, her worried frown visible from the top of the slope, one hand on her head in dismay at the state of me. 'Why did you let them do this again?' she asked. 'Why didn't you tell the teacher?'

But it was perhaps for the same reason that I'd bought them all gifts on holiday – because I wanted them to like me. If the Deaf Girl took one more beating, might this be the last, would they *then* start to like me? If I bought them presents from Spain, would they eventually see that I was just like them? Or would they smash them all up and stuff them inside my wooden desk for me to find at the end of the day?

I look down again at the shameful pile of twisted and shattered keyrings in front of me, as hot tears prick behind my eyes and sadness stings at the back of my throat.

Mam was right, I thought. *I should never have tried to befriend the bullies. I have to accept that some people are just cruel. Like Granddad said, they just don't have good hearts.*

I slam the wooden desk shut and dry my eyes.

And the bullying continues for another year.

Chapter Five

There comes a day in every bully's life when her victim says enough is enough. For me – that victim – today is the day.

I'm walking out of school in my black school uniform and grey jumper. My plastic yellow jelly bag is swinging in my hand and my schoolbooks are weighing down heavy inside.

Life has changed a lot in the last few months, mostly because I've started junior high school. I was so thankful to leave Oakfield behind me, and my first day at Breckenbeds Junior High School felt like a new start.

Breckenbeds is a two-storey modern school that stands beside the main railway line into Newcastle. Its playing fields are ringed by a heavy black fence which keeps us fearless kids away from the dangers of the train tracks. British Rail passengers, weary from announcements about leaves on the line, might be able to spot us hunched over our desks as they pass by our huge classroom windows. For our part, we've got used to the rumble of the trains, which often makes the floor shake beneath our smart, black school shoes.

The school is so big that we have to switch classrooms for different lessons. I feel very grown up as I carry my books from room to room, bustling along the silent corridors which are actually thronging with hundreds of noisy students.

I enjoy my lessons at Breckenbeds; home economics is one of my favourites. Each week I carry all my ingredients into school in a wicker basket; taking whatever we've made home for Mam and Granddad. I love geography too; my time on The Bridge at Oakfield standing me in good stead for knowing where's where in the world, as well as the hours and hours of speech therapy with Granddad naming capital cities.

Sometimes it can be difficult to keep up with what the teacher is saying in class, but at home after school I spread all of my books over our new smoky-glass dining table and pore over encyclopedias until I've taken in everything that the teachers have told us about that day – even if I couldn't hear it at the time.

Mam sees me working hard on my homework and I do put in a lot of effort, tracing pictures of Elizabethans out of our huge encyclopedias to copy into my schoolbooks, but for me, school is mostly about socialising. Victoria is still my best friend, but these days our little gang of two has swollen to include some new girls – Natasha, Beverley, Dawn – and the boys too.

In fact, boys are becoming a bigger part of all of our lives now. And our newfound maturity is stretching to include awareness of our own personal style, too. Long gone are the bunches I used to let my mum pull my hair into every morning; instead, I now want to wear it down like my new friends.

Except in typical teenage style, my hair never does what I want. It's blonde and frizzy after I insisted on the same perm as Julie, but it doesn't look as good on me as it does on her. She washes her hair and scrunches it dry with the big diffuser on the hairdryer; it's huge and curly, and set stiff with mousse that dries so hard and crunchy you feel like you could break a lock clean in half. But my hairstyle, especially with my fashion faux pas curly fringe, never looks as good as Julie's. Luckily, all of us are starting to experiment with clothes, hairstyles and make-up, so no one stands out too much among the throng of school uniforms that flood into Breckenbeds each morning.

School has got so much better for me here, mostly thanks to *Donkey Kong*. The fact that my hearing-aid batteries are the same as those that fit into the Nintendo game has meant that I'm a vital cog in the wheel of anyone stuck on one level when their handheld console dies on them. We're all playing it here at Breckenbeds, but it was the naughty boys back on The Bridge who first put two and two together that the batteries matched. It ensured I finally made friends back at Oakfield, and I didn't mind being plunged into silence if it meant one of us could reach the next level.

And yet, there is another thing that has followed me to Breckenbeds that I wish would have just stayed at Oakfield – my bully. A small fish in a big pond these days, her cruel jibes are few and far between, but there are often times when she can't resist the chance to remind me that I'm deaf. She might not have the same backing now we're all a little bit older and wiser, and she may have swapped long white primary-school socks for short ones, but she still has the same cruel heart.

For years, I have done what Mam and Granddad have said, I've let the taunts and even the beatings wash over me but, for some reason, today I am going to put a stop to it for good.

We're just leaving school, and as usual everyone is milling about, saying goodbye and gossiping about who got detention that day. Yet as we all prepare to scatter for home, there she is, up in my face, a twisted and dark look in her eye as she prepares to deliver another insult which she's dreamt up.

'Well, *I'm* going to go home and watch television,' she says. 'But *she* can't.'

Another dig, another reminder that, as I wave goodbye to all my friends at school, just like any other girl, I am *not* any other girl. I am different. And to some people, I always will be.

I can't describe this feeling, this pure rage that's bubbling up inside me now. I know that people call it a red mist, perhaps that's the most fitting description, because even though not a sound has ever penetrated my ears from this girl, I've heard enough from her.

I shove my jelly bag into one friend's hand, my coat in another's, and before I know it I'm marching over to her, and with sheer strength that I never knew I had, I'm dragging her. Her feet are scraping along the ground as she tries to keep up with my force, she's shouting, threatening me, I can tell each time I catch a glimpse of her twisted face, but there's no stopping me. I'm on a mission.

I drag her through the underpass, onto the grassy bank that's sheltered by trees on the other side.

My heart is racing as I throw her onto the ground, blood pumping through my veins. I know the other kids are egging us on; a crowd has followed us into the shady glen that's far enough away from the watchful gaze of teachers.

And then I start: punching at her, pulling her hair, strands of wispy brown hair getting tangled between my fingers. But still I go on, scratching, kicking, pushing, spitting.

She gives as good as she gets, but I don't feel anything as she lands another slap in my face. Adrenaline and years of insults have numbed me to any finger she might lay on me now.

The anger bubbles up and boils over like a cauldron that's been stewing with helplessness for too many years. Total and utter defiance replaces the fear that is pumping around my body.

'This is for when you called me a spastic,' I spit, as I feel my school shoe land against her rib. 'This is for when you made my Victoria cry,' I shriek.

Years of pent-up frustration come tumbling out in the form of violence. The punches and kicks continue until her blouse is ruffled and torn, and clumps of her hair blow softly on the ground.

How it stops, I'm not sure. Rage has somehow changed the sequence of time. I think she runs off, but I can't be sure. I am covered in punches and bruises, but I don't care. Because I'm tasting something more than just humiliation in my spit. For once – for the first time ever – I'm tasting power.

I have been on the receiving end of her blows for years; she has made my life a misery. But not anymore. This is the end. I am determined about that.

As I walk home, not even noticing my own blouse is torn, or

that my black-and-yellow school tie is hanging askew around my neck, the adrenaline is still pumping through my veins. More than anything, I feel satisfied that I've finally stood up for myself.

But as I turn into my road, the police car standing outside our house leaves me stock still for a second.

Mam is standing up in the living room next to a policeman when I walk in. He looks so official and alien in our tiny front room. 'I told you not to fight, Joanne,' she says, casting her eyes up and down over my ripped clothing and ruffled hair. 'I didn't want you to fight.'

'But Mam,' I plead with her. 'I'd had enough.'

I watch as she and the policeman exchange glances. I don't know then that Mam has already explained to him everything I'd been through at Oakfield, how we'd hoped Breckenbeds would be a new start.

And yet, in that single sentence, I'd said everything he needed to hear to understand the situation. The years of taunts, the days after days that I'd come home to get myself patched up by Mam. The patience I'd shown in the hope that something would change, that my bully would one day start to like me. Instead, finally, I'd snapped and they could both see it.

Of course the bully had lied, though. She'd injured her finger in woodwork that day, yet she claimed I'd done it to her in the fight. After everything I'd endured from her, the very first time I fought back, she ran off telling tales. But everyone knows that bullies are weak underneath the bravado.

The police officer sits me down. 'Sticks and stones will break your bones, pet. But names will never hurt you,' he says.

I look at him and think, *what do you know? Have you ever been bullied? Do you know what it's like to be born without the gift of hearing? Do you know how it feels to spend day after day attempting to live without the use of one of your senses and then being battered for it, both verbally and physically?*

Yes, it is true that I can't hear most of the names that are said behind my back, that I focus instead on the friend whose arms I've linked through, but just because I'm deaf doesn't mean I'm blind too. I see the hurt flash in my friend's eyes like a mirror to the bully who is standing behind me. When my friend tries to pretend that someone hasn't just called me a cruel name, I try to pretend too. But I see the way that people deliver their jibes, even if I can't hear them. I've become adept at picking out the faces that don't understand what it's like to live with a disability, who think that I deserve to be called names just because I'm not like them. I just choose for the most part not to take any notice. To think that it's a shame for them that they can't understand, or don't want to get to know me.

So don't tell me that names will never hurt you – because I can't hear them and they still do, I think.

But I don't say any of that aloud because he'll never understand. Instead, I nod. I can see the policeman is kind, and that he knows what I've been through, and I accept that what I've done is wrong.

I never have any bother from that girl ever again. And I realise something else that day: I might be just eleven years old, but I'm strong.

*   *   *

Something else changed when I moved up to Breckenbeds. My phonic ear was replaced by two tiny hearing aids. That big heavy metal box, which had weighed down so heavy on my chest and my childhood, was gone. Instead, two flesh-coloured bugs were fitted behind my ears.

How long had I wanted to shake free from the shackles of those thick red straps that pushed down on my shoulders and tied in a clasp at the back? To not be victim to someone behind me, pinging it free for a cheap laugh, and watching the whole lot clatter to the floor while the teacher turned round and sighed, exasperated?

And then freedom finally came when Mr Mathias told me I could just wear hearing aids. It wasn't because there had been any improvement in my hearing, but times had moved on. It was now 1986, no one was wearing phonic ears anymore, deaf children didn't need the stigma of wearing equipment as good as a warning sign that hung around their neck saying 'deaf'.

For me, losing the phonic ear meant looking and feeling like any other pre-teen girl. I looked like my other friends, and my school blouse instantly fitted better without crumpling under the weight. The fashionable clothes or plastic beads that I borrowed from Julie had previously been ruined by the clumpy accessory that none of my friends would be seen dead in. Not anymore. Now people could read the cool logos on the big baggy T-shirts I picked out with my pocket money. In short, I was finally like everyone else.

And yet, I was also unprepared for the fact that life without my phonic ear came with its own difficulties. It had never occurred to me that without something signalling my deafness around my neck, people often mistook me for ignorant when I didn't answer them or realise they were talking to me.

Supermarket trolleys would push into me, or scrape the back of my ankle because I hadn't heard someone asking me to move out of the way. It wasn't my fault that their calls of 'excuse me' had escaped my ears. And instead the sighs, the head-shaking, the mute insults from strangers became an everyday occurrence to me yet again. The straps from the phonic ear might have left my shoulders, and yet being without them forced me to grow another layer of thicker skin on my back, with which to let the insults wash over me.

So it hasn't been easy to get used to, but it has been worth it just to be able to dress like my friends for school in the morning. Finally, I am like everyone else.

But while I might have shaken free of the shackles of my phonic ear, I now have something else to take around with me instead: my note-taker, Mrs Brewis. She sits beside me in class, listening to the teachers for me and writing notes so that I can keep up with the lesson or catch up at home by going through them with Mam and Granddad.

But I hate the fact that having Mrs Brewis next to me instantly marks me out as different from my friends. While they all sit together on tables, giggling or passing notes, I sit next to her, forced to concentrate on a lesson that I can't even hear. I long for break time when I can find my friends and gossip with them about what funny things I missed out on in class, and who said what. When she's not there, I take the opportunity to muck about with my friends, to mark myself out as one of them once again.

Without Mrs Brewis, there's no one to tell me when my hearing aids are whistling and making my classmates giggle. Not that it bothers me if they're taking the mickey – I laugh along too because I've learnt the hard way that it's better to be liked for being different than picked on.

It's days like today though, when we have a relief teacher who doesn't know I'm deaf, that we get into the most trouble.

As we shuffle into the classroom, I'm oblivious to the excited chatter that our regular teacher is away and we have a supply. By the time the chatter reaches me, I know the drill.

I wander over to the window and place my hearing aids between the slatted blinds, then, trying hard to stifle a laugh as the whole class sniggers, I walk back and take my place at my desk.

I am plunged into a completely silent world, but scanning the faces of my classmates tells me all I need to hear. They are loving this practical joke.

The hearing aids must be whistling because the teacher is looking round the room, confused.

A hand flies up as one of the boys tries his best to say without laughing: 'Miss, what's that noise?' I lip-read his words as I snigger into my hands.

The teacher looks up, more confused than ever. She checks under the desk, the drawers, her handbag.

'Miss!' More hands go flying up.

We're all trying to stifle the laughter now. My belly aches from holding it in. I love moments like these when I'm in on the joke with my classmates, where I can actually be the bearer rather than the receiver of the laughs. These are the best times, even if I can't hear the giggles or my classmates goading the teacher about where the noise is coming from. Is it the door? Is it the fire exit? Is it the cupboards?

But finally, when we can stand it no more, and our faces are red from laughing on the inside of our cheeks, she finds the hearing aids hidden in the slatted blinds and returns them to me, her face set in a stony expression. Momentarily, I feel bad to have humiliated her, yet just turning round to the class and seeing the approving faces quickly replaces any guilt with a lovely warm feeling inside.

I am like my friends. I can be one of them. Long gone are those Oakfield days now.

And even Mrs Brewis, it seems, has her uses. A few days later we have a test, and when she sees us struggling for the answer to one question she quickly scribbles it down on a piece of paper and flashes it to me and a few of my friends.

In an instant, she becomes our classroom ally.

I leave school that day part of the biggest secret that we'll be talking about for months. Finally, I'm on the inside, in on the joke, fully inside the hearing world, actually *making* the joke, rather than always the outsider looking in.

We're sat on the living room floor beside our hi-fi, the glass door is open and Julie is putting on one LP after another. As her friends dance around the room to Wham, I put my head right up to the speaker.

The girls' eyes are sparkling with delight as they bop up and down in time with the music, they giggle over the routines they've choreographed in their bedrooms, and sing along to all the words that they've spent hours learning. They've listened to this LP over and over; they have the lyrics down to a tee. I can only tell because they all sing in unison, their mouths moving in time, never missing a beat between them.

But still I stay on the floor, my ear pressed right up against the speaker as it blasts out 'Everything she wants' yet again.

Why am I here? Because I'm desperate to hear something, anything. I want to learn the words so I can sing along too. I want to delight in this deep throaty voice that the girls tell me he has. But all my hearing aids are picking up is the dull and distant thump of the bass.

In that moment, I long just to be able to climb inside this speaker. To be inside this sound. If I were in there, could I dance like Julie and her friends? Could I delight in the songs like they do? Would I be able to learn all the words too?

I want to be a part of their lives, wearing Duran Duran sweatbands simply because I love their music, not just because everyone else is wearing them.

I want to be able to look at each poster that is plastered around Julie's room, and know what each of these different pop stars sounds like.

I want to have a soundtrack to my teens, or even know what it feels like to have one. Instead, I press my ear a little closer into the speaker, desperate for something, anything, always sure I'm just one note away from hearing.

There's a *buzz* . . .*buzz* . . .*buzz* . . . a tempo I can pick up in my ear, but anything else is a muffled white noise. But I quickly learn that's all you need for a beat to dance to.

Julie tries her best to help me learn the words to sing along with them. She'll tape-record *Top of the Pops* and pause, rewind, pause, rewind, until she's written down all the lyrics for me. In years to come, she'll mouth along the words to Right Said Fred's 'I'm Too Sexy' because she knows that's one of my favourites. With his deep deep voice, I can just hear a distant echo of lyrics, but it's something, a taste of what these girls have.

Unlike them, I've never heard Christmas songs. I don't walk around department stores in December hearing those same old favourites; there is no musical trigger for me to know that Santa is on his way. I can sometimes make out the distant twinkle of bells at the start of 'Last Christmas'. They're so faint it's frustrating. But it's something: the only Christmas song I can say I know.

Julie and her friends spend a lot of time around this hi-fi in Mam's living room. A lot has changed in here over the years. The wall has come down between the hall and the front room, and an arch has been built in between the two reception rooms. The walls and ceilings have recently been artexed, and Mam will often sit on the sofa in the evening, admiring how trendy it's all looking. Our brown furry sofa has been dispatched to Granddad and in its place is a new posh mink corner sofa that us girls like to lie on, feet up, in front of cartoons after school, while Mam constantly reminds us to take our shoes off first; I only know because I see how quickly Alana jumps down each time and unbuckles her own T-bar pair. The smoky-glass dining table, complete with metal-framed leather chairs, hasn't been here that long, neither has the white sideboard with its pull-down drinks cabinet. Alana and I raid the cocktail cherry jar inside while Mam's in the kitchen; and when they or Julie have friends over, we like to play with the porcupine cocktail-stick holder.

Alana is eight now and still so much fun, she'll play for hours with her Slinky on the stairs, watching delighted as it coils down every step, one at a time. In the summer, she's always clutching a Screwball dripping with strawberry sauce – or monkey's blood, as we call it. She'll beg me and Julie to time her as she races round to the sweetie shop on Dartmouth Avenue on her bike. We never do, but as soon as Julie hears her dashing back into the house she'll start counting: '. . .106, 107, 108! Wow! That was really fast!' And Alana will beam, her cheeks shiny with sweat. Even though me and Julie are older we'll spread the Twister mat out in the garden, or the living room on colder days, and I'll have to lipread the colours that Granddad calls out as he watches us tangle ourselves in arms and legs.

Julie has a Saturday job these days and she spends her money on clothes from Sergeant Peppers, a clothes shop in town. She wears baggy dresses with tight skirts and big thick belts, and denim jackets with the sleeves rolled up. I copy her and think she looks so cool.

She'll spend hours taping songs off *The Chart Show* and listening to them over and over again. When Mam calls up to her in her bedroom she often doesn't hear because her music is so loud. I watch Mam sigh and march up there to let her know tea is ready. Granddad laughs about it: so it's not just me who can't hear Mam . . .

Two years later, at fourteen, I move from Breckenbeds to Heathfield Senior High School to study for my GCSEs. Here we're mixed in classes with older teenagers; we sit at long wooden desks sometimes equipped with typewriters. Everything smells wooden in this school, from the science labs to the gym hall with its shiny polished parquet floor.

Student art lines the corridors between our classes, but here it's much more professional than the pieces I've seen at my other schools; it looks like it's been plucked straight out of an art gallery.

Photographs are proudly scattered everywhere of pupils with their Duke of Edinburgh awards. The school is very sporty – there are always several games of football going on at any one time in the school fields – so it's no surprise to learn that many Geordie footballers who played for England once walked the same corridors as I do now.

I make new friends here; Allison, Emily and Ashfiya are my closest confidantes these days. We wear our black-and-blue stripy school ties short and fat in an attempt to make our school uniforms look a little more cool.

Ashfiya is probably the only one of my hearing friends who really knows how I feel to face prejudice in my life; because her parents are from Bangladesh, she has been subjected to cruel comments too, only, unlike me, she hears every single one of them.

Once, we'd popped to Greggs for our usual lunch of a cheese-and-onion pasty. As we walked up the street back to school, we scrunched up our paper bags to take shots at the bin. We were only playing, but when Ashfiya's missed the bin and rolled across the pavement, one man didn't think she was going to pick it up.

'Get back to your own country,' he snarled at her. I saw the hurt sting her eyes, and I know full well the pain that jabs at your heart, then swims around for hours later in your tummy. It was my turn then to comfort her.

These days, I'm not constantly trying to prove to myself that I'm a normal teen – because I am one. I kiss boys, I drink when I'm not supposed to, and I still get detention for talking in class. But even if my deafness isn't noticeable to me, it is to others.

Often I'll get home from school and take off my jacket to find white pools of spit on the back of it. I haven't noticed some of the lads on the top deck of the bus spitting on me when I got off. I haven't heard their accompanying jibes either. But the thick skin I've developed means it doesn't get to me. There will always be mean people in the world. I've learnt that it's up to you whether you pay any attention to them or not.

The fact that my ears don't work has always meant that I have been forced to focus on the people who *do* matter. This has become my philosophy for life.

And it's one I'm very happy with.

Chapter Six

My head feels like a lead weight, my eyelids too heavy to blink. And yet as I try to open my eyes – slowly, very slowly – I see a strange room come into focus. Stark white walls, and stripped lighting zigzagging across the ceiling. A disinfectant smell instantly hits my nose. There's no white noise, only silence, which means someone has taken away my hearing aids. My eyes scan my bedside for them, and as they do, they land on a familiar face: Mam.

She's sitting beside my bed, wearing the same worried frown that I've seen so many times before: when I'd staggered home from school bloodied and bruised; when she'd found me lying in the road after being hit by a car; when I fell off my bike.

Despite the fact that my head feels as if someone has stuffed it full of thick cotton wool, my heart immediately lurches for her. What have I done this time, I wonder.

But before I can ask, Mam has turned away hurriedly, to beckon a doctor over to my bed.

When she turns back to me, her worry lines seem lighter already. She's reassured to see that I've woken up.

'Joanne,' Mam mouths to me. 'Are you OK?'

It's difficult to tell. My body feels tired; it's hard to figure out where each individual limb ends and the NHS mattress I'm lying on begins. I try to move my arms and legs, but they feel more like pieces of wood as I manage to shuffle them only a few inches.

'What happened?' I ask Mam, trying to get up onto my elbows and failing, before flopping back down.

'Just relax,' I see Mam say, as she reaches out to touch my forehead and the doctor takes a torch out of his pocket and shines it into my eyes.

'You fainted,' says Mam, beyond the white of the torchlight.

Fainted? But how . . . ?

And then, slowly, my mind starts to piece together some pictures. Walking home from school with my friends Allison and Ashfiya . . . The July sunshine beating down on us . . . No school uniform because we're on study leave – we'd only gone into school that morning for a maths lessons . . . And then, blackness. Nothing. Until I woke up in this bed with its hard metal frame fencing me in.

As my brain makes sense of what I remembered, dropping those images into some kind of order, Mam fills in more blanks for me. She tells me how I'd fainted in the street outside a local butcher's, how they'd rung for an ambulance before calling her.

She's been sitting here for ten minutes, waiting for me to wake up. Again the worry lines seem fainter than before, but they're still there – made a little deeper, I imagine, by each minute she'd sat beside my bed, praying for me to wake up.

'What can you remember, Joanne?' Mam asks. But there's nothing out of the ordinary; there are no clues to help the doctor figure out why I passed out in the middle of the day. One minute I'd been walking down the street, the next I was here.

Mam looks puzzled. I watch as she glances at the doctor and spot their matching frowns.

'Can you remember anything else at all?' The doctor asks me, as he picks up my limp wrist to take my pulse. It feels so heavy within his firm grip.

I shake my head.

I'm sixteen now and this is the first time I've ever fainted. There is no explanation for it. I see some words like 'exam stress' and 'hormonal changes' leave the doctor's lips as he tries to comfort my worried mam, but he seems as puzzled as any of us.

I search between the pair of them as I watch their silent conversation. I'm just as confused as they are.

But there's one word that crops up over and over again, the same shapes forming between the doctor's lips, and it's one that I don't recognise: 'Usher'.

Mam repeats it because it's new to her too, and as the doctor explains a little more to her, her worry lines seem to deepen again. And I see him mention another word: 'blindness'.

I lie stock still in my bed, unsure on whether I've picked up the right parts of the conversation. My heart is beating harder in my chest as my eyes frantically dart back and forth between their faces as the two of them stand over my bed like characters in a silent movie hospital scene. Yet this isn't fiction, this is my life, and nothing could have prepared me to see a word like 'blindness' leave anyone's lips in relation to my health.

The doctor leaves and Mam sits down.

'What did he say?' I ask her.

She tells me that he mentioned Usher Syndrome. All we know right now is that it is a progressive, genetic condition that causes blindness as well as deafness. Without both of those senses in full working order, it can cause balance issues, so the doctors want to run tests to see if it could be that.

'But it probably isn't,' Mam quickly says.

Yet however hard she's trying to put my mind at rest, she forgets that I've become an expert at reading little telltale signs from her: it's how we've managed all these years. There's a dark fear in the back of her blue eyes that only I would be able to pick up on, even if I can't hear the falter in her voice.

She's trying to stay matter of fact, trying to be positive, but my sixteen-year-old teenage mind is whirring with questions and fears. They're rolling around my head, one after another, spilling into my ears, my nose, my throat. I swallow hard and now they're churning away in my tummy.

Blindness. Could I be going blind? I blink and look around the room. I *look* around the room. You see? I can't be blind: I can see. The mound of my feet under the sheets at the end of the bed. The doctor's notes that are on a clipboard hanging on the bedframe. And finally back to Mam's face.

'But you probably haven't got it,' she tries again, this time with a light smile which I know is deliberately for me, and something inside me starts to believe her – because if I can *see* her lips moving as she reassures me, if I'm watching her right now in front of me, how could I possibly be going blind? Of course not.

But over the next few days, the doctors do more and more tests. Medical students file in one after the other to look into my eyes, pulling back the curtains that afford me the teeniest bit of privacy on this busy children's ward, flashing a torch into my pupils until lights dance around the room in front of me, stealing any ability I have to lip-read, and remaining there long after they've left to move onto another 'exhibit'.

They treat me as if I'm just another case in their textbook, like I'm nothing but a lump of flesh to them. I feel humiliated as a group of them talk over my bed, unable to keep up with the conversation, with the medical terms that spill from their mouths quicker than my brain can catch or decipher.

They're talking about me, and I'm desperate to know what they're saying, but the lack of sound to fit the shapes of the words that tumble out of their mouths makes it impossible.

The student doctors shuffle off on their rounds, and I lie in the silence, looking at my hands, my feet, the busy ward. I'm not blind. I *can* see.

Yet they seem to be the only ones who can't see that.

I'm standing in a nightclub and I've never felt so alive in all of my life. Music pumps through me, pounding through my feet, my legs, my chest, my head, in between my ears, my throat, even the backs of my eyes.

It's like I've climbed inside one of the speakers in Mam and Dad's hi-fi. As if it has swallowed me up, just as I'd always wished, and now I'm in here, floating about weightlessly in sound, right inside the song, the beat in tune with my own heart – or at least it feels like that to me.

I imagine the lyrics are swirling in ribbons around me, but if I reach out to touch one, they disappear like a puff of dust. I can't catch the words, I can't hear the tempo, but I have the beat and it picks me up and carries me along with it. This is what music *feels* like to a deaf person. The vibrations that come through the floor, the walls, that pump through my veins as much as the blood that carries oxygen around my body.

It's dark in this club, so dark and smoky you can hardly see your hands in front of your face, but every few seconds a flash in the darkness will light up the scene, filling it with people dancing, waving, jumping to the beat, just like me. The lights colour in the sounds that escape my ears. Strobes flash and dance in time with the beat, and I can move with it, I can dance because I can feel it. I can *see* the sound. The drums play inside me, and my feet move in time.

I feel electrified, excited, alive inside this nightclub for the first time in my life, like nothing I've felt before.

You might wonder why a deaf person would go to a nightclub. If you can't hear music, then what's the point, you might think. But that's the thing about nightclubs: you *feel* music. I don't need to hear the lyrics when the beat itself is coursing through me.

If you could see me now, you wouldn't have any idea that the girl in the middle of the dance floor – waving her arms, moving her feet, all the time with a huge smile painted right across her face – was deaf.

I am in Kavos in Corfu. Julie is nearly twenty now and she's been working as a travel agent for the last few months. We've come away on holiday for my first trip abroad together, and we're determined to do nothing but party.

In previous years I'd always felt the age gap between me and Julie. She and her friends seemed so grown up compared to me and my friends, but, recently, the four years between us haven't seemed too huge. Julie is like one of my best friends now, and that's how we find ourselves here.

We spend the days sunbathing, playing beach volleyball and jumping off the side of boats on diving day trips.

Kavos is the party capital, one long street full of nightclubs, and bars serving two-for-one drinks and cocktails in fishbowls. No one checks my age here, not like the bouncers back in Newcastle, where you need to memorise your star sign, remembering to knock a couple of years off your date of birth.

And here I'm not the Deaf Girl either. I've never had any problems meeting lads back home in Gateshead – I've always been chatted up and had boyfriends – but most people know I'm deaf before we've even got chatting; they've more than likely seen me around, or a friend might nudge their elbow to tell them when they catch them checking me out. I'm used to my disability putting me on the back foot before I've even started up a conversation.

But here in Kavos, lads come over to chat me up in nightclubs as if I'm any other girl. I'm not the Deaf Girl, I'm me, Joanne.

Ironically, though, just recently, even I have accepted that I *am* the Deaf Girl. I've spent my whole life desperate to be like everyone else, wanting to pretend that I'm not deaf, but the doctors back home frightened me with their suspicions about Usher. They are still doing tests, and as we prepare for each hospital appointment Mam tells me over and over that it might not be Usher, but it's always there at the back of my mind. Even standing here in the darkness of this nightclub, there are split seconds when I wonder whether this might be my future. Will the colour fade out of my life, trickle away just like the sound?

But I've got used to pushing any fears to the back of my mind. I'm not blind. I'm not going blind. Not until the doctors tell me, I've decided.

Yet it's always there, that nagging fear.

But it's changed me in another way: it's made me embrace being deaf. I don't need to pretend I don't have this disability. It's making me determined to live every single minute of my life, squeezing the fun out of every hour. How many other teenagers can say the same?

So when lads come over to chat me up in nightclubs, instinctively leaning towards my ear, I tell them straightaway: 'I'm deaf, I need to see your lips.'

In hot and sticky nightclubs, I have an even playing field. No one can hear each other; everyone is relying on lip-reading to a certain extent.

If I see someone I like across the dance floor, it doesn't matter that I'm deaf when it comes to us locking eyes. The fact that we're thousands of miles from home and have had one too many two-for-one cocktails running through our bloodstream is a good thing: it gives us the confidence to start chatting.

So much is said in the smile we exchange across a dance floor, or the way we radiate towards each other as we start to dance. The unconscious messages that I rely on day after day without my sense of hearing are heightened in here under these disco lights, amid the music that's blasting out of speakers and making it impossible for anyone else to hear.

Perhaps they know how it feels to be me now. But instead of too much sound making communication tricky, it's too little.

Whenever we're in a bar, knocking back brightly coloured drinks decorated with tiny paper umbrellas and glitzy straws, Julie is never far away from me. I know, whoever she's talking to, she always has one eye on me and my conversation.

Whenever someone keeps leaning in to whisper in my ear, she'll pull them back and remind them that I'm deaf.

'She needs to see your lips,' she'll say.

Julie has always looked out for me, so it doesn't bother me when she explains to them. I've got used to her gesturing to me with her eyes that someone we know has just walked in the room in case I haven't noticed them arrive. Or giving me that raised eyebrow and wide-eyed expression, a secret code between us that says, 'Look cool, someone is checking you out.'

And of course there are the ones who are put off by my disability, there is always someone who wants to knock your confidence, but this is where the thick skin I've grown over the years comes in useful. Because the ones who don't want to talk to me once they know I'm deaf are not the guys I want to talk to either. I don't hear the nasty jibes because I'm deaf to it, physically and meta-phorically. I'll only know that something's going on when I catch Julie saying: 'It's you that's stupid, not her!'

Like Granddad always told me, it's what's inside your heart that counts. So I always concentrate on the people who do want to be nice to me.

And in this nightclub, where no one knows any different when they spot me across the dance floor, I am just like any other girl.

I know I'm not, though. I'm deaf.

And these days I'm proud to be, and feel my deafness to be a part of me, the way I am, rather than a disability.

Alana is peeking between the bannisters on the stairs, Mam is sitting on the sofa, and Julie is standing beside the phone with me, but we're all trying desperately not to giggle.

'What did he say?' I mouth to Julie.

'He says he's in love with you,' she mimes back at me.

And there we all go again, in fits of giggles: Alana rolling around on the stairs; Mam clutching her tummy and trying not to make a sound; and me and Julie, the tears of laughter rolling down our faces.

I take a swipe at her. I know she's making it up and that this poor lad has only called to arrange a date. Goodness knows what he's thinking on the other end of the line.

He must have been brave to pick up the phone and call me for a date in the first place, knowing he wouldn't be able to speak to me direct, but would need to go through my sister or my mam.

I'm sure most people take using a phone for granted, particularly when it comes to arranging a date, but for years I've got used to the loudspeaker phone in our living room and the fact that the whole family listen in on my conversations, articulating whatever my friend is saying on the other end so that I can answer.

It never used to be embarrassing when it was Vicky, or Allison, or Ashfiya on the line. We knew to save our private conversations for when we're face to face. But with lads calling, it's a bit different now.

There are some guys who are put off by that. I'll give them my phone number when we say goodbye on holiday, or at the end of a night back home in Newcastle, and when I explain that not only do they need to call my house, but that someone will need to translate for me, I see the confusion cross their brow, a moment of uncertainty in their eyes. And of course, there are guys who don't call, the ones who don't want to have to say everything through your mam.

Then there are the ones who *do* call and are quite happy to talk to Mam – in fact, they never seem to hang up!

But the most embarrassing times are when the boys I really like call. It's at times like those that I wish I could hide behind the sofa to take a call in private, so my mam, Julie and Alana wouldn't see my face blush as I answer them, or how my heart is beating out of my T-shirt.

Most of the time a lad calls, though, it's like this: Julie taking the mickey and telling me they're saying things that they're not.

The four of us girls stifling silent giggles and doing anything we can to arrange where to meet and to get him off the phone as quickly as possible, so that once the receiver is down we can laugh and laugh about it.

Dad barely looks up from his paper while us girls are in fits of giggles. As the only man in the house, he's used to us. I think he just feels sorry for the boys on the other end of the line.

This is one of the happiest times of my life – not just because of the attention I'm recieving, but mostly because of the fun I'm having now. Dad doesn't work away any longer, and Mam seems happier to have him around more. He's a constant in our lives, giving us lifts to our friends' at the weekend, always taking me to hospital appointments, and whenever me and Julie are off some-where sunny he'll take us to the airport. Dad has always been a quiet man, and with four women in the house, he's never got a word in edgeways anyway. But he loves his family, that I've always known, and he is fiercely protective: on family trips, lads aren't even allowed to talk to us on holiday; his stare alone is enough to put them off. He'd do anything for us. Within reason.

Since leaving school, I've got a job working as an admin assis-tant in an office on the Team Valley, the local retail park. I can do everything there – typing, filing; the only thing I can't do, of course, is answer the phone. My colleagues are lovely. Unlike when I started school and faced prejudice and bullying, I've found it's nothing like that in the working world. People are only too happy to help me learn in the office: it's no big deal that I'm deaf, they work with me to make things easier. Each Tuesday, I have a day release to college to study for my BTEC diploma in business studies. My favourite time in the week is chatting in the staff room at lunch and getting to know everyone.

But, really, I live for the weekend.

Goodness knows how I find the money, but I'm out both Friday and Saturday nights in town with my friends. Since my trip to Kavos, Julie and I have been on more and more cheap holidays through her work.

Back home, my friends and I spend each weekend in clubs in Newcastle: Powerhouse and Rockshots and The Boat, an old cruise ship that's since been turned into a nightclub, complete with a revolving dance floor. The only problem with it is when you spot a friend in the crowd and you have to wait until it goes round again to get off and say hello.

Nightclubs are where I feel most at home. I instantly recognise songs when they come on through the beat alone, which courses through me. I spend whole nights just dancing, in my long hippy floral dresses and Doc Marten boots, and drink pints of lager.

Wherever we are each night, Julie and I will meet up for last orders in Bigg Market, ready to catch the last bus home together from Worswick Street Bus Station. Everyone piles on, and it's always such a laugh as we all sing on the 25-minute bus journey back to Gateshead.

Julie and I will fall off the bus, usually picking up a few stragglers as we head back to the Chowdene estate. Mam and Alana – who is twelve by now – will still be up watching telly when we wander in with friends we've met on the bus, who had further to walk home than we did and fancied warming up first. Alana loves to hear about our nights out, just like I did at her age when Julie started going to clubs. Mam never minds the friends that we bring home to chat to at the kitchen table, while she makes us all cheese on toast and serves packets of crisps with cups of hot steamy tea, which warm us up after the walk home.

Dad is always in bed, but Mam and Alana will sit and chat with us all, getting all the gossip from the night, not realising it eventually becomes 3 a.m.

If I bring one of my boyfriends home for a cup of tea, I'll catch a glimpse of Alana's face as he puts his arm around me and try not to laugh.

I'm eighteen now and these are the happiest times. Julie and I went to Faliraki in Rhodes a few months ago and made some great new friends. About ten of them came to my eighteenth birthday party a few weeks ago, and Julie had one final surprise for me: a Tarzan-a-gram turned up in nothing but a loincloth and whipped me off my feet and over his shoulder.

It's times like this, up in the air, over the shoulder of a half-naked man that I – quite rightly – forget anything about the Usher tests, which are still ongoing.

In some brave moments, I've dared to pick up a leaflet on Usher, or look at a book about it. But any posters I see of blind people at the doctor's surgery or in the hospital scare me witless. They are always photographed with these blank expressions: looking up, looking down, but never at the camera that they clearly can't see. They always look as if they're struggling and unhappy in the picture, lost in the world around them. I picture them with a white stick or a dog to get around, or worse with a carer, and I think, *that can't be a flash-forward to my future. It looks so sad to be blind.*

Not when I'm here, now, getting ready for a night out, putting on my thick black eyeliner with perfect precision, checking my reflection in the mirror, and brushing my long blonde hair, which falls all the way down my back.

I don't ever want to turn into one of those people in the posters. I want to stay me.

I'm having so much fun that I can't imagine a time when I won't be able to laugh it all up, to see these smiling faces, to be out in a club being chatted up by a guy.

But if the doctors are right, if I really do have Usher, that might well be my future.

And however much fun I'm having now, that cloud is always hanging over me.

Chapter Seven

'OK, it's your turn,' Paul says, egging me on.

I'm sitting in the garden of the Hunters Moor Hospital. I have been working in the library here for the last six months, and I love it.

The contrast between my quiet nine-to-five job, and my weekends spent nightclubbing, couldn't be more stark. If I could hear the dance music that accompanies every one of my weekends, it would still be ringing in my ears come Monday morning. Mam says I enjoy myself so much that even if I dropped dead at twenty-one, I'd have had a fantastic life.

This is the second library assistant job I have had since completing my business studies course, and it's my favourite.

Hunters Moor Hospital is a specialist neurological rehabilitation unit, set in a beautiful old Victorian building. I take the winding path up to the main entrance every morning, walking through a beautiful garden filled with rose bushes and an oak tree that has stood in the same spot for hundreds of years. Old photographs of the hospital in the 1920s line the corridors, and you can see that oak tree standing tall and proud in them, like a loyal soldier guarding his battlement.

This place used to be a leprosy colony in its previous life and patients and staff say the walls are haunted by its former occupants. There are plenty of creepy stories about the place, but I find its history comforting, the haughtiness of the building pretty, and my favourite place of all is the garden where we're now sitting.

'Well?' Paul says, pushing me to answer him.

I clear my throat to start. 'There's a beautiful peach rose bush beside us. The leaves are such a vivid green, their edges hard and jagged yet at the same time they look as soft as a feather. Tiny little veins fan out like hundreds of fingers from the stem of the leaf, and out of the thorn-covered stalks grow the most wonderful flowers . . .'

I glance over at Paul. He's listening, but I can see he's losing interest. I try again to keep his attention. 'The rose is made up of layers and layers of petals blossoming out from the centre. Inside it's the deepest colour, and most tightly woven bunch of peach, yet the colour fades as the petals spread and open out into the sunshine . . .'

Paul is shuffling in his seat.

'Is that it?' he says.

'It's beautiful,' I try again, but his mind is not for persuading.

'OK, your go,' I say.

He closes his eyes. 'I can hear a beautiful bird singing in a tree above us, its song is as gentle as raindrops on your skin, each individual note twinkles in the breeze, enough to bring a tear to your eye yet it's such a beautiful cheery song. The little bird never tires, just sits alongside us, tweeting his happy tune about summer and worms, and the tiny nest he's been building within the branches . . .'

He pauses. 'OK, your turn . . .'

Paul and I can sit here for hours like this, but of course we don't because we're at work. Paul works alongside me in the general office at the hospital reception. His main job is to answer the phones, as it's clear that I can't. But then he can't file the books away or search for a medical encyclopedia one of the doctors has requested, because Paul is as blind as I am deaf and, for that reason, we make a pretty good team.

I'd been working at the hospital for three months when Paul – and his black Labrador guide dog, Gary – joined. We instantly had an easy relationship; I could talk to Paul about his disability as easily as my own. He became my ears and I became his eyes as we described what was happening around us each day.

'What does the boss look like?' Paul would ask, and I'd describe her, right down to the flip-flops or what drink she was buying at the bar.

'They're asking if you want another drink,' Paul would tell me, as we sat having a shandy over at the pub across the road on a Friday lunchtime. And I'd shout back, 'Just a half of lager,' without anyone who didn't already know me knowing that I hadn't heard a thing.

But it's this conversation we constantly have on repeat: is it better to be deaf or blind? Paul and I will take turns describing

93

something I can see or something he can hear. He is determined it's better to be blind; I say the opposite. And yet somehow, as Paul describes a soft-rock ballad that he's just discovered, or something as simple as a bird song that I've never had the pleasure of listening to, he always manages to make me feel like I would be better with a working pair of ears than my eyes.

If I describe a new pair of shoes I've bought and the pleasure of seeing them on my feet, he'll sigh as if I've got no idea how the wonder of listening to music or hearing a friend's voice could trump my latest fashion accessory every time. He'll insist I don't really know what music sounds like, despite my protests. 'That's just the vibrations,' he'll say, tapping a tempo on my knee. 'That's not *hearing* music, that's just your concept of music.'

And he'll keep going, keep asking me for another narrative into the world that surrounds him and yet one he's never laid eyes on. Paul has been blind since birth, all he sees each day is black, perhaps some blurry shadow at the corner of his world. He'll often twist and turn his face for a glimpse of movement or a whisper of something that my eyes take for granted. And yet – just like me and my ears – it always escapes him.

'Your turn,' he says again.

I take a deep breath, determined to win the blind/deaf argument this time. As we sit under the great oak tree with some of the patients, my eyes fall on one in particular.

'A smiling face,' I tell Paul. 'The way someone's whole face lights up when they laugh, the way their eyes crinkle at the side, and their irises dance with delight. The way their nose wrinkles when they find something really funny or their mouth breaks into the most wonderful grin, revealing all their happy white teeth . . .'

I pause and glance over at Paul. He's listening to every word. He reaches out and finds my leg to tap to make sure I'm looking at him; it has become second nature to the pair of us to take into account each of our disabilities in order to communicate.

'I would like to see my mother's face,' I see him mouth.

Instead I take his hands and let him feel around my face. We've done this before. He gently strokes the side of my cheek, brushing the back of his hands against my long blonde hair. His fingertips find my nose, my lips, my chin.

'You are just as I imagine,' he says, leaning back again.

Paul tells me that, just as when you're reading a book you imagine what each character looks like, he does the same.

'Do I look nice?' I always tease.

'Oh yes,' he grins.

Granddad will often ring the office and speak to Paul, usually to ask me what I want for my tea if I'm visiting him that night. Anyone who knows me knows just how important Granddad is and has always been in my life. Now I'm working, I make a point of going to visit him once a week for tea. We'll sit and chat just like we always have, his eyes sparkling as I tell him about my day at work.

Being an ex-army man, Granddad is very traditional about what he serves up for tea, and he especially loves anything from a tin. He'll ring the hospital and leave a message with Paul for me asking what I'd like and the choices are always the same: beans and sausages or Big Soup. He serves it with thick-cut white bread which is slathered in Stork margarine, and melts under the heat of whichever tinned delight I've picked out for that evening. It's always the same choice for dessert, too: tinned Devonshire custard with either pears or prunes.

There have been times when Granddad hasn't been well enough recently to get to the shops – old age has caught up with him – and my Auntie Val and Uncle David will ask me if I'd like a lasagne or something different for a change. But I don't like to disappoint Granddad, so I'm always happy to have beans and sausages or Big Soup.

When Granddad calls with his never-changing menu, he'll always stay on the phone a bit longer to have a chat with Paul. He's always been interested in my friends and their lives, and even though I'm now 21, he'll still ask me what I fancy for tea.

Paul is just one of the reasons why I love it here at Hunters Moor. There are other things, too: the eccentric professor who pads around in bare feet, the doctors and psychologists I've befriended, and of course the patients.

It's also where I've had my first real experience of death. Just a few weeks ago we had a social evening for the patients and staff in one of the communal rooms. I got chatting to a lovely man who was on one of the wards. We chatted and laughed as he sat there in his striped pyjamas and tartan dressing gown. He must have only been in his fifties, clearly a very kind man, but he was one of the long-term patients here. We had a little raffle and as he hadn't brought any money along, I offered to buy him a strip of tickets along with my own. During the evening, he fell poorly and the nurses had to take him back to the ward. The following morning, it turned out that his strip of tickets had won the raffle. Delighted and excited to be giving him his prize of a box of chocolates, I went up to the ward to find him. But when I arrived, his bed was stripped and deserted. He'd died in the night.

I couldn't believe that someone who had seemed so full of life and laughter just hours before could be gone so quickly. But it was experiences like this that made those of us working at Hunters Moor realise just how precious life is.

So when the long corridors of the old building are deserted at teatime, the staff race each other up and down them in wheelchairs, whooping and laughing as the wheels skid along the polished floors, the breeze whistling past our ears.

For the poignancy of my debates with Paul isn't lost on me. The doctors still haven't ruled out that I could have Usher. Might I one day be like Paul myself? Blind – as well as deaf?

That's why, as one of the nurses on a well-deserved break prepares to race me down the corridors in our matching borrowed wheelchairs, I'm loving every minute . . . in case one day I can't see any of this anymore.

I'm lying flat on my back. I open my eyes and see that familiar, stark strip lighting criss-crossing above me and curtains pulled round my hospital bed. I look down at my side and spot my friend Jo, one of the psychologists from the hospital. The worry etched across her face reminds me so much of Mam. I reach out a hand to comfort her. I don't need her to tell me what's happened, as I already know – I've fainted again.

This time it was at work. For almost four years now I've been free of hospital appointments. I've been living my life, loving every minute of my job all week, and every second of my weekend. The longer life went on without another hospital appointment, the more sure I became that I didn't have Usher, but it was always there, in the back of my mind. And then life has thrown me back into this hospital bed, under the watchful eye of the doctors who will once again shine torches into my eyes until they momentarily blind me with their glare and leave me unable to lip-read anything they're saying to me.

This time, when a doctor comes to see me, Usher is one of the first words that leaves his lips. The tests proved inconclusive before, but these ones are bound to confirm it.

Day after day, they keep me in hospital. I don't need to be here, I feel fine. But they want to do test after test; they take blood, tissue, even give me a lumbar puncture. On the third day, they wheel me into a lecture theatre and put me in the middle of the stage. I wrap my dressing gown around me that little bit tighter, feeling so exposed sitting there, despite the fact that I've got my nightie and fluffy slippers on too.

As the consultant addresses a team of medical students, I have no way of knowing what they're discussing. And one after the other they take their turn to examine me. The torches that they shine into the back of my eye leave my eyeballs screaming for some shade; by the time they've finished my eyes feel angry and painful, the lights still jumping in front of my eyes and my ears plunged further into darkness because their experiments alone have left me blinded by the light.

When the glare has faded, I see one say that Usher is a genetic condition, that it can be inherited. I've always pictured myself with a husband and children; as kids ourselves, Julie and I would often pick out names for our imaginary offspring. Yet I feel so angry, so exposed as I sit here at the mercy of these students more used to poring over their books than dealing with real people, that I vow I'll never have a child if there's a chance they might be treated like this if they've got Usher too.

At home again a few days later, Mam and I don't speak about the future. When she'd turned up at the hospital, her chest heaving with those deep sighs I'd become so familiar with throughout my childhood, we'd just exchanged a look that said we knew it had to be Usher.

She knew there was no point in telling me it wasn't, because I don't even need doctors to tell me it is now. I know in my bones. I might be going blind.

I go through every scenario in those two weeks at home, while the doctors assess more and more samples. As I apply my make-up each morning, I wonder, how much longer will I be able to do this? Will I need help getting dressed? How quickly will it happen?

I think of how much I love my job; how I enjoy those nights out with new friends I've met in clubs like Powerhouse and Rockshots, particularly with my lovely friend Sean. The flash of the strobe lights, the way they light up the happy faces every few seconds before plunging everyone into momentary darkness again. Catching someone's eye across a dance floor, subconsciously deciding in those few seconds that you fancy them.

That would all go.

And so would any kind of conversation – because without my eyes, how could I lip-read?

All of life's colour would be replaced with blackness and silence.

My mind flashes back to those images I saw in books and magazines: the blind people who looked so lost in their world. There have been times when Paul has made me think that it wouldn't be so bad to be blind – but only if you have your ears. Without either, who would I be? Not me, that's for sure. I can't bear to lose sight of my friends' faces, smiles to strangers on the bus, flicking through old photographs and remembering those wild holidays with Julie or Alana pulling a silly face to make me laugh.

My friends from work come round to visit me at my mam's. One professor, who's always been convinced I have Usher, promises me they'll all be there to support me.

And then, finally, I am called in to see the consultant. Mam comes with me, and as we sit down at his desk, he starts shuffling through some paperwork while my stomach ties itself in knots that feel as if they could reach up into my throat and choke me.

'Well, it's good news,' he says at last, breaking into a broad grin. 'You haven't got Usher.'

After that, his words all blur into one, because the tears that were already welling in my eyes wash them all away.

Mam and I stumble out of his office a few minutes later into the round open waiting room, and I burst into tears.

'What are you crying for?' A nurse smiles at me. 'It's good news.'

The waiting room is crowded and people are looking at me.

Mam takes my hands and leads me out of the automatic doors, but on the street it is raining so we are forced back inside.

'It's good news,' she laughs, wiping away my tears.

But it isn't for me, because I just *know* I have Usher. It doesn't matter what the results say; I know in my heart that it is Usher and no one is going to convince me otherwise. I've lived in the shadow of this syndrome for the last six years, I've told myself I probably don't have it as many times as Mam has, but it is always there. And these last two weeks have convinced me that I had been right: I'd lived my life as I'd known it and now it would all change.

We step back inside the automatic door, and heads go up to see us back in the waiting room.

'You haven't got it, Joanne,' Mam is saying. She is smiling at me, holding my face in her hands.

'What do I do now?' I sob. 'Just go and get on with my life?'

'Exactly that,' she says.

And we fish inside our handbags for umbrellas and step out into the rain and the streets of Newcastle.

Everyone at work is so thrilled for me when I tell them it isn't Usher. My desk is decorated with brightly coloured congratulations cards that make me feel uneasy somewhere deep down inside.

I tell myself that it is only the result of living in the shadow of Usher for the last few years that is convincing me the doctors have missed something. But there remains this nagging fear, this worry that there is something wrong. I've been freed from those shackles by the medical professionals, and yet I am keeping myself prisoner by remaining so convinced that the tests are wrong.

But how can they be?

Yet just the fear of losing my sight has changed me. Just living in the shadows of what might have been for two weeks has made me think about what life would be like without the independence that Mam has fought so hard to instil in me.

So while everyone at home and work is still celebrating on my behalf, I decide to make some big changes in my life.

The first and biggest decision I make is that I want to be a nurse. It has always been my lifelong ambition and, fortified by the news that my life is my own again, I am determined to make it count. I also feel like I could make a difference. I've been to the edge and looked over; perhaps my experience will give me some insight when it comes to helping others.

I find out what qualifications I'll need to stand a chance of getting accepted to study nursing at university and, over the next two years, I make it my mission to get there. I work hard in the day at Hunters Moor, and study at college in the evening to get the two A levels which will get me a place at university.

I pore over books and fill in one application form after another to get on the course. I get the place I wanted, and in the few weeks before I start a four-year nursing degree, I make numerous trips to the city to get everything I'll need: a brand-new leather satchel, numerous ring-bound folders in which to store my notes, a new pencil case filled with biros. When I pick the pens up, bristling in their Cellophane packets, I smile to myself, remembering how Mam had encouraged me as a child to keep two sharp pencils in my case, to avoid being sent to The Bridge.

But this wouldn't be like that. Going to university wouldn't be like starting a new school with that anxiety welling in my stomach about who might not like me because I'm deaf, or what cruel jibes I might receive.

At twenty-three, there is no need for Mam to come and explain to my teachers that I need to be able to lip-read their lessons, or to make numerous trips to the headteacher to complain when the teachers ignore her request.

So as I stand outside Newcastle University, watching hundreds of students file into their classes in front of me, there is no anxiety in my stomach – only excitement.

We spend the morning in lecture halls, hearing about the modules we'll be studying in our first year. I can't wait to start writing notes up in my brand-new files.

Lunch is spent in the university refectory, getting to know some of my new classmates and sharing our hopes for the future. Most people admire the fact that I want to specialise in an audiology department or work with deaf children. I've never seen myself as an A & E nurse or on the wards; I wouldn't be able to work there with my disability. But I believe I could at least work in the community, or as a practice nurse. I am determined that I can help people by spreading deaf awareness.

In the afternoon, we meet another lecturer. I try not to be put off by the fact that he has a very angry face as I introduce myself to him, explaining that, as I lip-read, it would be helpful if I could sit at the front so I can watch him speak to us. He asks me what sort of a nurse I am planning to be. I explain my hopes of working with children or in an audiology department, but whether he is busy or flustered by all the new students, he doesn't seem convinced.

'Do you think your deafness could hold you back?' he asks me.

'Not at all,' I say, proudly.

I've spent my whole life having to explain my disability, so our exchange doesn't worry me too much. Nevertheless, as I take my place among the rest of the students sitting on tall stools, I know he might need some persuading about my abilities.

As the lecture starts, though, he seems to forget my request to watch him at the front of the stage. As he explains more about our modules with him, he skips around the room, weaving in and out of the other students.

My head turns from one side to the other, left to right, trying to keep up with him. But he is making it impossible for me to follow him – and he seems to be enjoying it.

Realising I've lost him among the students, I stare straight ahead, waiting for him to come back to the front of the class, but instead I notice that everyone is staring at me. It is hard to read the looks on their faces; some of them might be staring in pity, others horror. I turn around quickly to see why they are looking at me, and there is the lecturer standing behind me.

'What did I just say?' he asks me.

I shake my head. I don't know.

'See?' he says, lifting his hands up to the other students as if the case is closed, his point made.

The student next to me obviously feels for me. She tells me he's been standing behind me saying 'Nurse! Nurse!', as if he were a patient on a ward trying to get my attention. But, of course, he knew I wasn't going to be able to hear.

The tears are already pricking at my eyes and before I can swallow them, they spill down my cheeks and onto my desk.

I gather up my new satchel and my books and run out of the room. I leave the university and head straight for the Metro, for home. I cry all the way, not so much because he's humiliated me in front of the whole room, but because I've clearly humiliated myself by even attempting to be a nurse. What was I thinking?

At home, I tell Mam and Granddad the whole sorry story. They'd been so excited to hear about my first day. Instead, I tell them how that lecturer was right: I'd been stupid to even think that I could be a nurse.

In the days to come, the university call home. Obviously someone has alerted them to what has happened; they apologise and say it won't happen again.

But it is too late for me. I gave up on my dream there and then. I didn't blame that lecturer as much as myself.

I never go back to university after that first day. Mam begs me to, she knows how excited I had been, how much work I'd put into it, but eventually she accepts my decision.

'You can be something better than a nurse,' Granddad tells me.

And I vow that I will be.

Chapter Eight

'Now remember: mirror, signal, manoeuvre.'

I watch what my driving instructor, Eric, is saying intently, before turning back to the steering wheel and the clear, straight road ahead. Before we set off he gives me instructions on where to drive to; once there we'll pull up and have a chat about how I've done. There he'll tell me where I went wrong and what I did right, because obviously it's impossible to hear him when I'm staring straight ahead at the road.

I get ready to pull away. Strapping my seatbelt around me, I push it into the holder and pull back on it to make sure it's fastened. I've noticed that my driving instructor doesn't do this; he just pushes it in without even looking. Perhaps there's a noise to let you know that it's secure? But, of course, I don't know.

Next, signal. I flip my indicator up with my left hand, searching the dashboard for the green flashing light, then once I find it I put the car into gear, check over my shoulder and I'm off – albeit to a chugging start as I take my foot off the clutch too quickly. I lurch forward in my seat, but soon I'm driving, crawling along the road, other cars passing beside me as I focus my entire concentration on the tarmac ahead.

Since I was given the all clear for Usher Syndrome at the hospital, I've decided to embrace all the things I feared I'd never be able to do – and learning to drive is one of them.

Eric picks me up from work twice a week, and I drive us home to Gateshead, pulling over for tips every few minutes. Perhaps it's a slower process than he's used to with other students – after all, he can't call out to me while my eyes are on the road – but he never makes me feel flustered or hurried, and he's very patient.

As for me, just the feeling of being behind the wheel, of being in control of my own destiny, is reward enough at the moment, however slowly I'm learning.

The driving lessons are just one of the changes I've made in the last few months. Since that terrible experience at the university, I've also got myself a new job, and I passed my driving test first time round some months later.

It was hard to pick myself up again after such a great disappointment. I sat around at home for seven weeks, long rainy afternoons spent sat inside, scouring the *Chronicle* for jobs. But then one day I found this one, Project Officer at an organisation called Tedco.

Tedco offers support to businesses and those who want to get into work in South Tyneside, specifically people with learning disabilities. My job is to organise disability awareness courses for local companies, as well as equipping people with the skills they need to get into work, and I absolutely love it.

In fact, our disability awareness courses – which I work on alongside my colleague, also called Jo – have become so popular there's now a waiting list to join. It is the late nineties and the government has been taking a particular interest in helping disabled people get into work – and part of that includes educating those who will work with them.

My job is to teach employees simple things like: never stand with your back to a window when you're talking to a deaf person, as the light will cast a shadow on your face and make it impossible for them to lip-read. Always make eye contact with a person in a wheelchair rather than the person who's pushing it. And how to offer help to a blind person if they appear to be struggling to cross the road or drop their shopping, when otherwise they might be going about their day quite confidently.

I guess I've been used to all my friends being around me and learning to make certain allowances, but it's still incredible how little tips like these can educate people and make employing disabled staff a much easier task.

Here at Tedco I really feel I'm making a difference; perhaps more so than in any role as a nurse. I can see the change in people as their confidence grows with each session, how they learn to put together a CV, or to make eye contact during interview practice. It's not just skills for business that we're equipping people with, but we're giving them confidence, too.

But over the weeks I see people who at first come shuffling through the doors blossom and bloom, and every Friday I leave the industrial estate where I work so proud of how many people I've been able to help that week. And I've made a friend for life in Jo as we become the duo Little and Big Jo.

And this is just the start. I'm only twenty-five, but I already know that my passion, my real calling, is to help others. However much life has moved on for me since I faced the threat of an Usher diagnosis, I still can't shake off that feeling that my life could have stopped as I knew it, right there and then. I can still close my eyes and remember the fear I had that the light would go out in my life, that as easily as I can close my eyelids now, the smiling faces around me would disappear, and so, with that, would any kind of communication.

Mam and I have also started going to British Sign Language courses in the last six months, yet sometimes I sit in those lessons and feel like I don't belong at all. I've waited until my mid twenties to learn sign language and so it feels completely alien to me.

I've always straddled two worlds, not really fitting into either. Mum has always been so determined for me to be a part of the hearing world, and for that I am eternally grateful. But in the hearing world I was the 'deaf girl'. Most of the time, people said that with pride. If they spotted me dancing, grinning, 'lost' in music on a dance floor, they'd nudge each other and say, 'Can you believe she's deaf?!' If they spotted me singing along to a song that someone had taught me, they'd be astounded.

All my life, people have asked me how I can speak so well. 'How do you have a Geordie accent if you can't hear?' I've been asked too many times to mention. I'm still not sure how to answer.

But the truth is I've never felt any different from a hearing person. And yet I think back to when I was two and I had to wear that phonic ear, how that firmly marked me out as different – until I reached the deaf unit. Then I was just the same as everyone else because we all had phonic ears.

And that's why I'm here now. I'm wondering whether I should try to be a part of the deaf community, whether that's a part of my identity that I haven't embraced fully. Is it a missing piece of me?

I copy Julie, the teacher who's signing, as I watched fascinated by its beauty, but it doesn't come naturally to me. It's only afterwards, when the whole class descends on the pub, that my signing skills start to pick up. There, socialising with people from the class and some BSL users who would join in to help us, learning why each and every one of them wants to learn how to sign, I get the practice I need. I learn a lot about deaf culture in those days and also met Mike and John, who were in my class, with whom I would go on to have good friendships. I never feel part of the deaf community, but with the friends I made we have always supported each other's individual circumstances.

And knowing how to sign really is useful in my role at Tedco when I'm dealing with BSL users, or even for teaching basic deaf awareness to those who work alongside someone who's deaf.

My job at Tedco means I'm making a difference every day. I'm helping people who might be living with the fears that I only experienced for a couple of weeks, who might feel the world – and therefore their options – are closing in around them. By teaching their colleagues a few bits of sign language, I'm opening up a conversation for them in the office, so they can explain what they did at the weekend instead of sit working in silence.

And it's at times like these that I remember what Granddad said, that perhaps I would be something better than a nurse.

I love my work at Tedco, but I know this is only the beginning. I've recently applied for a role that would involve helping people on a national scale. It's as Regional Officer for Radar, the Royal Association for Disability and Rehabilitation. If I got this job, I'd be the 'voice' of disabled people across the whole of the north of England to central government.

I tell Granddad all about it when I go to visit him at the nursing home he's moved to. He's very frail these days but his blue eyes still sparkle as I tell him how my interview went.

I tell him what a big role it is, how hundreds of people are applying from all over the country.

'You'll get it,' he tells me, lifting a shaky hand to pat me proudly on the knee. 'I know you will.'

I hope he's right.

It's hard to recognise the tiny man whose head peeps out from beneath the pristine sheets of the little single bed. His face looks so small nestled into that pillow, his skin sunken into cheeks that were once pink and full of life, but he hasn't eaten much for weeks, despite everyone's attempts to encourage him. Just last week, I bought Granddad some of his favourite pear drops, but when I popped one into his mouth, it clattered around noisily in his jaw, and he screwed up his nose.

A combination of old age and the cancer that has been eating away at his kidneys for the last few years have finally taken its toll on him.

Gone are the days when we used to drive up to see Granddad on a Saturday morning to take him out for a pub lunch at the pub next door. It was the highlight of his week when he'd first moved to this nursing home in Northumberland.

We'd march into his room and he'd be sitting there in his wheelchair, all ready for us in his overcoat and beautifully polished shoes. His hair perfectly combed to the right, a faint whiff of Imperial Leather in the air and eyes dancing in the sheer delight of me, Mam and Dad coming to visit.

As we sat down in the pub for lunch, he'd tell us how he'd been deciding what to have all week, before settling finally on scampi and chips and a half of lager and lime.

He was always so interested in what we'd been doing. I'd tell him about my work at Tedco and he'd always remember to ask after some of the learners I'd told him about. More recently, I'd been telling him about going for this Radar job; last week I'd told him I was down to the last two. This week I have even better news . . .

Back in his room, everything has its place. How on earth he's scaled down from the house he once shared with Grandma to the little box room he has now, I can't begin to imagine. What happened to a lifetime's worth of possessions?

These days he doesn't even have room for a coffee table. In his last place, at the sheltered accommodation, he'd kept all his daily essentials lined up on the coffee table in the middle of the room: letter opener, glasses, pen, address book, shopping list, packet of polo mints, playing cards. He constantly had bruises on his legs from walking into it, but as he knew I was clumsy too, he'd laugh about it and make me feel better by rolling up his trouser legs to show me the purple and green landscape of his own shin.

Yet there is one item that is so precious to him, it has pride of place wherever he goes: the picture of Granddad surrounded by all of us grandchildren. It has never left his side in all these years.

In that picture, he is just as I remember him from when I was a child. Strong and proud, gentle but firm, the apples of his cheeks always rosy from skipping down the street with us kids, or laughing at one or another of us showing off.

The picture prompts me to remember the walks we used to take to the bus stop together: my hand in his giant palm as he sang 'Danny Boy' to the little deaf girl who cantered along beside him, trying to keep up with his huge stride. I recall the hours he spent poring over my schoolbooks with me, or lining up five-pence pieces and only sliding one over to me once I'd pronounced 'Berlin' properly or whatever exercise we were doing that day. It was never a chore to sit there with Granddad after school while Julie or Alana skipped in and out of the house with various friends on hot summer's days. I was just pleased to have him to myself.

And today I realise, with pain in my heart, that our time together is not infinite. It is time to say goodbye to Granddad. Julie and Alana have already been here this morning to say their own goodbyes with Mam, and now it's my turn.

As I kneel down beside his bed, there is still one unmistakable thing about the weakened man who croaks out a hello to me – those lovely blue eyes. They haven't lost their sparkle altogether, but today they look dull and glassy, as if it's an effort to keep looking out at the world which will soon vanish before him.

But although they may not have the energy to dance for me today, the warmth in his gaze is still undeniable.

'I got that job.' I smile at him. I'd just heard by letter that morning. I am now the regional officer for the north, a big job that will see me travelling the whole country, standing up for the rights of disabled people.

His eyes crease at the side, just for a second. 'I knew you would,' he tells me.

Although I can't hear the effort in his voice each time he speaks, I can see how weak he is; his lips hardly move as he speaks, and the smile which has been his face's constant companion is replaced by a fatigue that is impossible to disguise.

'Thank you for everything you have done for me, Granddad,' I say to him. It is from the heart, a moment that I can't let pass me by because I know this will be our last chance.

I know just how much I have to thank him for, not only the hours and hours spent sitting with me and doing my speech therapy, not even the interest he's always shown in anything I've done. But the positive attitude, the kindness and empathy he's instilled in me. At 26, he's made me the person I am. How can I not thank him for that?

A fat tear falls softly from his blue eyes, slowly tracing a line down his cheek. I haven't noticed the tears pouring from my own eyes. Granddad's hand comes up from under the covers and brushes at the teardrop on his cheek. It is only then, when I see that big strong hand of his against his tiny face, that I realise how frail he's become in front of my eyes.

This man who has meant everything to me is about to leave us and he knows it, and my heart is breaking.

We are both crying now, silently acknowledging the fact that this is the last time we'll ever exchange words. I know that Granddad is slipping away from me – and yet I've never even had the simple pleasure of hearing his voice.

I get up to leave the room; Mam and Dad and my cousin Andrew are also here to say their goodbyes.

I reach the doorway and turn around to blow him my last-ever kiss. 'I love you,' I call to him, as the tears roll down my cheeks.

I watch him shake hands with my dad, and Mam gives him a kiss, and then we drive back to Gateshead, me and Mam with our arms wrapped around each other in the back, and Dad silently driving us away from Granddad.

We know it won't be long now, yet none of us could bear to have to say those words.

That night, I am meant to be going out to a casino with Julie, but I can't face going.

'It'll take your mind off things,' Mam insists.

So me and Julie get dressed up and go out with our friends, but we spend the entire night talking about Granddad. Every time I close my eyes I can see him, so tiny, in that hospital bed. But I am so happy I've been able to tell him my news. I know I've made him proud.

When I pad downstairs in my slippers the following morning, I find Mam sitting alone in the kitchen. I look at her, and she looks right back, and in that instant I know.

Granddad has gone.

I retreat back upstairs, overwhelmed by grief. Sitting on my bed, I pull a photograph out of my purse. It's a silly little thing really, and yet it means the world to me. A few years before, I'd found Mam putting a picture of me and Granddad into a frame. He's holding me in his arms; I'm about two years old. Mam had to trim it to make it fit the frame, and on the floor I'd spotted one of the off-cuts. I'd picked it up and that's what I hold in my hand now.

A tiny shiny piece of photographic paper, not much bigger than a postage stamp, shows my tiny toddler hand in Granddad's. Those strong hands that had lifted me up as a child, that had picked me up when I'd fallen or wiped away tears. That had slid those five-pence pieces towards me or clasped themselves together to celebrate one of my achievements.

Granddad had meant the world to this family, but to me, he had meant everything.

Big gothic arches carved out of honey-coloured limestone, ornate stonework covering every square inch of wall and topped with a panelled wooden ceiling that towers above little old me. Everything about this building packed with history, right down to the leaded windows, is beautiful.

I'm standing in the Members' Lobby at the House of Commons in London, next to a bronze statue of Sir Winston Churchill – just one of the many great names who have walked this stone floor before this blonde deaf girl from Gateshead.

And as I stand in this magnificent building, marvelling at the beauty and history of it, and reaching down every few seconds to pinch myself that I'm actually here, the one thing I keep thinking is that Granddad would be so proud if he could see me now.

My work with Radar means that I'm a regular visitor to London and the House of Commons these days. As regional officer for the north, my job is to represent disabled people to parliament. Radar is an umbrella organisation and just in my patch alone I am responsible for eighty-one different groups. If a deaf woman in the north of England needed an interpreter to help her give birth, then I will know about it – and make sure that central government knows if she was denied one. It is all about teaching society that disabled people are not incapable; it is the world around them that is making them incapable. So if one supermarket doesn't have a door wide enough for a wheelchair to fit through, or it has steps at the entrance rather than a ramp, it is their fault for not making their store accessible for disabled people. It's about raising disability awareness. Goodness knows the number of times I've sat in an audiology department and someone calls my name, 'Joanne Milne', falling on deaf ears.

Since passing my driving test, I go up and down the region in my little green Ford Ka attending meetings from the Midlands to the Scottish border. I love the independence that I have when I get in my car and zip down the motorway, or step off the train at King's Cross Station in London. I have also moved to Sheffield recently. The person I'm dating lives there and as a lot of my work is based in Yorkshire, it makes sense to be there rather than in Gateshead.

It's times like these when I really feel that I have come so far. If things had been different, I might be at home with Mam and Dad, struggling to communicate, and closed to other opportunities. Instead, here I am, getting on the Tube in London, or jumping onto one of those famous red buses. I feel like I'm linking the deaf and hearing worlds.

And I'm representing all those people who might not be as fortunate as I am. I'm working every day to make it a more inclusive society and want to ensure everyone has the support I was fortunate to have.

My job is very varied. I will sometimes hear of a deaf man who's just started a new job and feels isolated at work because his colleagues don't know how to communicate with him. In that case, I organise some deaf awareness training for the people in his office. Or if there's a restaurant that doesn't have a specially adapted disabled toilet, or a train which doesn't have signs in Braille, or if there are not enough blue badge parking bays outside a supermarket, or there's a second storey of a clothing shop which doesn't have a lift – I am the one who gets the government to listen.

It has been four years now since I was told I didn't have Usher, but I still can't shake off that fear I had that one day I might go blind, that all the things I now take for granted just like anyone else might disappear, quite literally, before my eyes.

I feel very strongly that I can help people, and that the voice that I was equipped with through hours and hours of speech therapy has a purpose now. It doesn't matter to me if I'm speaking to a visually impaired lady in her home in Gateshead, or an MP at the House of Commons. This is my job: to express the views of people who aren't in a position to reach the top.

Because that's where I am now. At the peak of my career, flying high, just like Granddad always said I would.

And I couldn't be happier.

Wedding of Ann and Al, March 1968. Featuring both sets of parents. (James and Mary Milne and Doris and William Moore.)

Ann Moore and Alexander Milne. Byker, Newcastle upon Tyne, 1963.

My arrival, July 1974.

Caravanning holidays in Berwick-upon-Tweed, 1982.

My first school picture.

Me with my phonic ear.

The class at Lindisfarne, 1980. Mrs Jackson is in the middle on the left, and Mrs McLellan is in the middle on the right.

On the swing in the back garden. Alana is on Nana Mary's lap.

Sisters celebrating New Year's Eve, 1986.

Holidays in Salou, Spain. August, 1986.

With Ashfiya, my best friend
when I was 16.

The last picture taken of me
with my grandfather.

On holiday with Julie in Kavos, 1991.

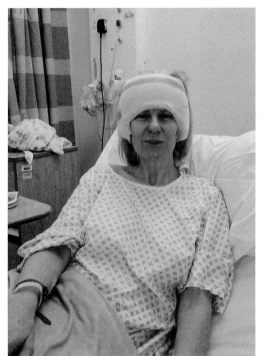

Hours after surgery at the Queen Elizabeth Hospital in Birmingham, February 2014.

With Richard.

With Aunt Edna, flying over the Grand Canyon in Las Vegas.

At the Hearing Fund UK gala
with Geoff, Matthew and
Luke, who all have microtia.
The two nine-year-old boys
are sponsored by HFUK to
take music lessons.

With my mum and
Merrill Osmond.

At a gig with my
friend Jo in 2013.

Giving a speech
to raise deaf
and deafblind
awareness.

With Angela, Deborah and Janvier.

With Tremayne, who compiled the Memory Tapes playlist, featuring 39 songs – one for each year of my life.

L-R: Janvier, me, Angela, Tremayne, Deborah and Aidan (Angela and Tremayne's youngest son), August 2014.

With Matt, trekking for Sense with Large Outdoors in the Peak District, September 2013.

Celebrating my 40th birthday in July 2014.
L-R: Mum, my cousin Lisa and her husband Geoff,
me, my school friend Emily and her daughter Emma.

With Alana, summer 2012

With Julie, weeks after the switch-on.

With my niece, Casey, Julie's daughter.

Chapter Nine

The room is in complete darkness, and yet there is one thing that I can still see – a pair of lips. If I close my eyes now, unable to lip-read, I'd have no idea what sweet nothings might be being whispered to me in the darkness. I'd just feel the wisp of hot breath against my face, or the gentle touch as lips meet mine, a thousand tiny nerve endings tingling inside me.

I feel the touch of hands on my skin, each hair tickling and bending under a warm palm, making me shudder with pleasure, and I momentarily close my eyes, to drink in this feeling even further, of two bodies so close, so warm, becoming one.

But without being able to hear, I keep my eyes open so I can see what's being whispered to me, to see those words – 'you're beautiful' – to look at the mouth that's telling me over and over again.

So how do I see this pair of lips in the darkness? You might be surprised to learn that a deaf woman has to learn many tricks even for something as simple as bringing my date home after a Christmas party. The Santa hat that I'd picked up because I was tipsy has actually proved quite useful; it has a flashing bauble on the end, and as it falls over my neck, resting on my collarbone, it lights up the lovely compliments that I'm drinking up like wine.

Perhaps people don't give too much thought to how a deaf woman might go about making love to someone. But, just like everyone else, of course we long to feel a body against our own, and the pleasure of making love to someone we fancy like mad.

I've made sure that being deaf has never held me back in any other aspect of my life, so why would it in regards to relationships either?

Sometimes, though, even I have to admit that it does make for some funny moments. I of course don't hear the thump of clothes as they hit the ground if someone has undressed without me knowing; instead I turn around and get the fright of my life. Or if I'm showering, facing away from the bathroom door with my eyes closed under the soapy suds, I might not notice someone's coming to join me until they've opened up the door and stepped swiftly into the spray. Any hearing person that I've brought home might jump out of their skin in the morning when the vibrating alarm clock goes off under my pillow. And oh, how I've often checked my cleavage thinking I'm alone in a room, when someone was sitting there all along.

I've learnt to laugh at these moments rather than feel embarrassed. When I've jumped out of my skin because I didn't hear someone undressing behind me, they've just joked, 'Surely, I don't look that bad naked!'

I'm twenty-nine now, and I haven't been single since I was seventeen. Love has always come easily to my life and my disability has never held me back. Relationships might not have lasted, but for the same reasons as any other woman, not because I'm deaf. In fact, my last relationship was with someone Dutch, which just goes to show that language has no barriers when it comes to love.

There's only one thing I have noticed recently, and that is that I'm finding socialising harder and harder these days. You might not find me on the dance floor of a nightclub anymore; more likely I'll be sitting in a wine bar or outside on a pavement cafe in Haarlem or Amsterdam. I tell myself it is because I'm not 18 anymore with boundless energy, but the truth is I find it hard work as I bump into people, then tables and chairs as I make my way to and from the dancefloor, my eyes failing me in the darkness. It is a classic symptom of Usher to have night blindness.

And dancing isn't the only thing that's getting harder if I'm completely honest with myself. I still love my job working for Radar, but the journeys zipping up and down the motorway in my little green car feel more like hard work now. Often I'll go to pull out, failing to notice the motorbike that's been about to overtake me. Looking over my shoulder to check my blind spot now takes even more effort, and I noticed recently that I can't see the colour of my jeans as I drive along without glancing down into my lap.

And there's been other things, too: reversing into a parking space and not noticing the bin that's beside my car until I feel the *clunk* as I try to open my door. And this is happening more and more often these days.

I haven't told anyone else, but I can't shake the uneasy feeling inside.

Because I know what this is. I don't need anyone to tell me. The doctors might have run their tests, they might have satisfied themselves, ticked boxes, put my case to rest, but I know what is happening to me.

I know that my world is getting smaller. I can see that it's happening every day; the fact I have to twist that little more round to check before I overtake on the motorway, or the fact that I have to look down to see what jeans I'm wearing in the car, rather than catching a glimpse of them in my peripheral vision.

It hasn't always been this way, but I'm noticing it is more and more.

Perhaps at first I pushed it to the back of my mind. I didn't want to acknowledge that there was anything wrong with my sight.

If I closed my eyes, I could still see those images of blind people from the books. I'd quickly open my eyes to replace them with a sunny day, some flowers, my office. But all of these things are disappearing in front of my eyes now. Tiny toddlers too close to the floor don't come into my view anymore, just their elder siblings. I'll feel so guilty when their mam picks them up; I must have seemed like I was ignoring them.

Because the truth is, I am going blind. I know it now. I don't need tests from the doctors, I don't need Mam telling me it's not Usher, because I know for myself. I 'see' it every day.

I do have Usher. I just know it.

Carefully I separate my long, blonde hair into three sections and start to plait it over my left shoulder. My hands know the drill, they've done this countless times before, so as if working on auto-matic, taking up their places for a dance they know so well, they intuitively start to separate the sections of hair, working and weaving, threading and turning, over and under, over and under, like the intricate footwork of a tango, until I feel the plait pulling my hair together at the base of my neck.

There's a rhythm and a grace to this, I think, as my hands work of their own accord, *a beauty in something as simple as plaiting my hair.*

Then I wonder: how many other women notice something like this as they dress in the morning? How many other women might lose the ability to see the plait come together, to be able to check the work their fingers have done so seamlessly?

I feel my throat tighten, and hot tears threaten to well in my eyes. I look at my perfectly made-up eyes and swallow the tears down, feeling my throat eventually relax and widen again. *Not yet, not now.*

The thick black eyeliner that I've been applying each day since I was a teenager, flicking the kohl out into a cat's eye, has been done with perfect precision. So too has my dusty pink blush and the slick of glossy peach that I've dabbed onto my lips. How much longer will I be wearing make-up? When will even my reflection disappear from this mirror? I swallow hard again. *Not yet.*

And then I take a familiar place in front of the mirror, shoul-ders back, facing forward, and – as on so many mornings over the last few months – I do a little test.

I'm wearing a Breton top made up of navy and white stripes.

Staring into the glass, I can see quite clearly: my face, my hair, the tops of my shoulders . . .

I place my hands in front of my tummy and start to wiggle them, then slowly start to move them up towards my neck. I keep on staring straight ahead at my reflection the whole time. The reflection I see before me. But I can't see any fingers. Up and up they come, until finally I see the tip of my index finger appear in my view. I count down from my shoulders: three stripes.

I have an uneasy sinking feeling in the pit of my stomach, because three months ago I could see my fingers four stripes down my top.

But today is the day: there is no hiding from this any longer. I check what I can see of my reflection one last time, then I turn and my eyes scan the bedroom for my handbag. My eyes. See? They do work! I try to convince myself.

And then I'm off. I've decided to get the bus to hospital today. It's a Tuesday morning. Of course, I should be at work, but as there are only weeks left before Christmas, I've decided to combine this hospital appointment with an afternoon picking out presents for the family.

That will help, I tell myself. But my festive thoughts are lost amongst the anxiety that is knotting up my insides and blanking out anything positive.

Today is the day.

The bus journey to the hospital seems longer than I remember, as we weave through traffic, pull into bus stops and give way to cars before we pull out again. I want to scream at the pace we're crawling along at. Because now I'm here, now today has come, I just want to hear the news. I just want to be there.

I've been living in Sheffield for the last three years. I love the trams that zip through the city centre, how quickly you can get from the town to the surrounding countryside, my beautiful three-storey Victorian villa with its high ceilings and the garden I treasure and, of course, the warmth of the Yorkshire people.

These streets that were once so alien to me, so different from those back in Gateshead, are now home to me, and because I've moved here to be with the person I love, I've never felt that longing for home. Home is here. I know the short cuts I could take if I was in my little green car; duck down there, right at the end, left turn ahead, then onto the main road.

I look down into my lap to check my watch. If I was driving, I'd be there by now.

It had been a few months ago that I'd gone to my GP to tell him that I needed referring to an eye specialist. I told him about the blind spots I'd been noticing, the blanks in my vision, the toddlers that were disappearing from my view because they were too small to be included in the tunnel I now looked out of, and the mistakes I'd been making in the car.

And I told him too about my history with Usher, that it had been mentioned and then discarded. He must have been able to tell from my voice that I was unconvinced by the results.

But today is the day.

Finally, the bus arrives at the hospital. I wait for the elderly ladies with their navy tartan shopping trolleys to get off first. Most of them have a bag of grapes poking out the top, along with a bottle of Lucozade that they're clearly going to dispense to a patient they've come to visit.

And then at last it's my turn. I look down to check the path is where I think it should be as I step off the bus. Little things like this have become second nature to me now. I usually don't even know I'm doing it, but then today isn't a usual day.

Inside the hospital, it is clear I'm in a place equipped for the visually impaired. Bright yellow signs with black writing line the walls, leading the way to the Eye Clinic. Yellow arrows show the way on the floor too; I follow them instinctively, not because I need these visual aids, I tell myself.

As I arrive at reception and give my name, I take my seat alongside the other patients in the waiting room. But a quick scan of the room tells me that most of them are not like me; they are more like the elderly women who shuffled off the bus with their coats and woolly hats and shopping trolleys. I imagine they're here for their cataracts, or other age-related eye conditions. Not like me. None of them is twenty-nine years old; they're not dressed in a fashionable Breton striped top, red Capri pants and flat pumps. They are not here to be told that their eyes are soon to be robbed from them . . .

A nurse comes over and taps me on the shoulder, interrupting my thoughts. 'Joanne Milne?' she asks.

I get up and follow her. There, in a darkened room, my eyes are subjected to test after test. Light shines in. *Blink*. Liquid dye is dropped in at the sides. *Blink*. Another torch. *Blink*.

My pupils scream as the light dances in front of them. I can't see the nurse anymore as she writes up some notes; I wouldn't know if she's talking to me now and I find the blindness terrifying.

Then, suddenly, I feel her hand on my arm: she's leading me out of the room.

Back in the waiting room and the seats have filled up. More people, most of them over fifty. There's one young woman like me – but she has a badge on her; another nurse comes over to her; she works here.

They come to collect me again after another ten minutes. This time they take me to a room where they take pictures of my eyes. It's uncomfortable sitting with my chin resting on the stand, my forehead pushed up against the frame to ensure I stay perfectly still. My neck is aching, my eyes are tired, and once again I'm returned to the waiting room.

Once more I look around the room. Most people are in pairs. Old men with grey hair and wrinkly skin sit alongside their wives. They don't speak; perhaps after all those years of marriage the conversation has dried up. Or perhaps it's too quiet here; they don't want to be heard. Instead, they sit with blank expressions, staring straight ahead, fingering the sleeve of their jacket, or crossing and uncrossing their legs as we wait. And wait.

I didn't want anyone here with me today. I haven't even told anyone I was coming. This is something I wanted to do myself.

I don't know why. Mam has always been with me for every other appointment. Maybe I don't want someone chatting away next to me, telling me that whatever the results are it will be fine. Maybe I don't want to hear their positive gabble, or the small talk, or even them attempting to take my mind off it.

Because today is the day.

'Joanne?' A nurse is standing beside me now. She's holding my notes close to her chest, a file thick with test results, years of scribble from various consultants, and now, somewhere inside, there is the truth for me.

I follow her into the specialist's office. I sit opposite the consultant while the nurse hands her the notes and takes a seat in the corner.

The specialist flicks through my file. 'When did you last have an eye test?' she asks me.

I tell her about my history, about all the tests for Usher, about how I've been noticing blind spots for the last few months. I tell her the test I did that very morning with my striped top. She's reading the notes the whole time, she doesn't look up as my incessant talking continues, and then I pause because I spot something that I've seen before in books, something that momentarily takes my breath away.

It's a photograph that I always called mouldy oranges, because that's what it looks like. An orange retina with black spots dotted all around the outside, like mouldy spots on a citrus that's been left too long at the bottom of a fruit bowl. It's otherwise known as *retinitis pigmentosa* – a classic case of Usher Syndrome.

But this photograph is not in a book any longer. It's tucked into my file; it's a photograph of my eyes.

'What did you expect you might be told here today?' the specialist is asking me.

I stare at her, blankly, still trying to take in the image that she's pulled out of my notes.

She's speaking to me in medical terms now, I see the word 'blind' leave her lips, and 'usher', but I'm struggling to take it all in. She hands me a note, and some pamphlets. 'You need to contact social services now,' she says, before scribbling something in her notes.

And then my consultation is over. The nurse gets up from her seat to guide me out of the room. There is no time to ask questions; there are no questions to ask. I've come for answers and I've got them, but I still can't quite take in what I've just been told. I have Usher Type 2.

The nurse is taking my arm and leading me out of the room, then she's calling the name of the next patient over my shoulder. I know because I feel her hot breath in my ear, see her go to collect another file of notes. Shell-shocked, I shuffle towards the exit, clutching the paperwork that the consultant has just given me in one hand, my handbag and coat in the other.

I am shocked and confused. I look around me, then down at the leaflet I'm holding as I walk out towards the street. And then I see what the paperwork says. There is a big tick next to the words 'registered blind'.

I'm registered blind. *I'm* registered blind. I stand stock still.

I thought I'd been prepared for this day, but my eyes just stare straight at those two words, slowly taking them in as my brain scrambles to keep up.

I look up at the street in front of me, at the cars going by, the people walking in and out of the hospital, while I'm pinned to the pavement by an invisible Velcro that refuses to let go of my feet. If I can see all this, how can I be blind?

My eyes scan the next bunch of leaflets. *What now?* one of them is titled. I open it, and words like 'social services', 'cane training', 'guide dogs for the blind' pop out at me.

Something is wrong, this can't be right. I can't be blind, I'm not, not yet.

My feet are still stuck fast to the pavement, my mind racing this way and that. I've imagined this moment so many times before, dreaded it, and yet it never looked like this in my mind's eye – alone outside a hospital, unable to believe what I've just been told, or should I say hardly told.

And then I feel overwhelmingly angry. I've been treated so appallingly, with such little regard. My disability awareness training alone tells me that, but this rage is something more emotive, more human.

No one should be told that they're blind like that and then be discarded out into the waiting room.

Luckily, I have grown that thick skin over the years. I am perhaps desensitised to rough treatment from others – but what if I wasn't, what if this was the single worst moment of my life?

And then I realise: it is.

No matter how brave a face I attempt to put on it, I am now registered blind. I have Usher. My life as I know it is over, and it has been replaced by this piece of paper that I'm holding in my hand now.

I think back to this morning: taking my time to dress myself, to do my hair and make-up. What for? To be told this?

I'd planned to do some Christmas shopping after my

appointment, but my feet are still held fast to the floor. *Come on*, I tell myself, trying to move. But it is impossible.

Everything else that has happened to me I've bounced back from. But there is an uneasy feeling in the pit of my stomach, a raw pain, an acid that is already swilling away in there, threatening to eat me up from the inside out.

Why? Because I'm deaf, and my eyes are everything to me. You could take my legs, my arms, anything – but not my eyes. Not my eyes.

The tears are coming thick and fast now, one after another rolls down my cheek, splashing on the pavement beneath me, but I'm in too much shock to wipe them away. Out they pour, one after the other, as I stand perfectly still, clutching these leaflets, and the form that has changed my life.

Thoughts tumble around in my brain. I try to catch one, to stop the merry-go-round inside me of all the things I won't be able to do anymore. I think of my little green car, how I love to drive, love the independence . . . I'll have to give that up now.

You'll be OK, a voice inside whispers. And I feel one foot lift up from the pavement, then the other, then the first again.

I'm walking towards the bus stop to town. I'm going to go and do my Christmas shopping.

But every few steps it suddenly hits me again. Shopping? How will I be able to do that anymore? I won't be able to wander round supermarkets picking things off the shelf; my view of baked bean cans will be replaced with black, with nothing, with darkness.

You'll be OK. There's that voice again. So I get on the bus and sit beside the window, looking out. I watch the cars passing by, the streets that I've driven on hundreds of times myself. I see people going about their lives, no different from the moment they woke up this morning.

Except for me, everything is different.

Chapter Ten

I have always loved Christmas, but in my silent world without the carols or those familiar yuletide number ones from years gone by, which I see rolled out decade after decade on *Top of the Pops*, it is the sights and smells of this time of year that have always left their biggest impression on me. The feel of a cold and squidgy satsuma as a child when your chubby hand is searching around the bottom of your stocking for another treat; the chocolate smell that hits you as you rip open a selection box; the cinders of a real fire; brandy snaps in the hamper that Granddad used to bring us each Christmas Eve; the colourful fairy lights on the Christmas tree, which kept a twinkly watch over our presents long after me, Julie and Alana had gone to bed.

It was always such a sociable time of year in our house when I was a little girl, friends and family were always dropping in for a glass of mulled wine with Mam and Dad. I'd stand in the kitchen as Mam served it up to our guests, the dark and citrussy cinnamon smell curling all the way from the hot pan to my nostrils.

No Christmas was complete without a Disney movie; my favourite has always been *Mary Poppins*. Julie and Alana had paused it enough times to make sure I followed the storyline, but it was Dick Van Dyke who captured the heart of my childhood imagination; his smile, his cheeriness always seemed so fitting for this time of year. I smile as I remember Julie's friend, Gillian who lived a few streets away on Dartmouth Avenue, teaching me to say 'supercalifragilisticexpialidocious,' till I could say it perfectly.

More recent Christmases as an adult have been just as exciting. Victorian houses seem perfect for this time of year, and I decorate every square inch of mine. Back home right now, Father Christmas and Mrs Christmas are sitting at either end of the fireplace in the living room, their legs dangling down over the mantelpiece, a holly wreath is pinned to the front door, and a real fir tree stands 9 foot tall in the sitting room, making the most of the high ceilings.

And yet, as I shuffle through this department store, watching people shopping together for presents, their eyes full of the kind of delight mine usually would be, I feel absolutely nothing. It's impossible right now to acknowledge any hope or magical expectation that this season usually has to offer, because it has all just been taken away from me.

The leaflets that I'd been clutching when I left the hospital are now buried deep underneath the perfume gift sets that I've chosen for my sisters, and yet somehow they still burn a hole in the plastic Boots bag.

I'd been organised enough to write a shopping list and plot my route around town before I left the house this morning, but I walk purely on automatic from shop to shop, picking up gifts that would usually give me so much pleasure – and yet, today, I can hardly raise a smile for the cashier as she pops the receipt in my bag and wishes me a merry Christmas.

What will be merry about it? I think, as I scoop up the rest of my shopping bags from the floor and head home, barely registering the fact that my arms are already aching from the strain, and my cheeks are still prickling with tiny pins and needles from the shock of my earlier news. What will be merry about any Christmas from now on?

It has been hours since I was told I am blind and yet it hasn't even started to sink in yet. How can it, when I only have to walk down the street, spotting the ruddy faces of all the other Christmas shoppers, hurrying by to the next shop in a bid to escape the cold, to know I can't be blind?

Nothing has changed in my sight since I woke up this morning. Except something *has* changed. I've been handed another label: blind.

Merry Christmas indeed.

I head home on the bus and start preparing a shepherd's pie for the evening meal, but as I peel the potatoes, I watch my tears falling onto them and discard them along with the muddy skins. How can it be true? How could I have Usher?

Of course my mind flits back and forth to the conversations I've had with consultants over the years, the ones who told me the tests had come back negative. But now there is no mistaking the diagnosis because I've run my own tests. I know my vision is getting smaller, the tunnel is closing in – and yet seeing it in the mirror as you make up your face each morning seems a world away from someone ticking a box on a piece of paper registering you blind.

I guess it's because while it's still only in the mirror, you can ignore it. But there, in black and white in front of me – I glance over at the pile of leaflets on the worktop – it is unmistakably true. I am blind.

I say it again: I am blind. And more tears fall from these eyes that have betrayed me.

I lie awake in bed that night, a familiar body beside me, but I can't join them in sleep. If I'm honest, I envy my partner the peace after the news I shared this evening.

I blink in the darkness, but with the curtains drawn, not a stitch of light creeping in from the moon, I can only tell because I feel my eyelids moving up and down. So this is what it'll be like. My hearing aids are on the bedside table beside me. Once again I'm in a world of silence, the same one I've always slept in. But now blindness joins me, and she is an irritating sleep companion, the worry and stress of her stripping me of any ability to be carried away into an unconscious slumber.

Every now and then, I'll look out into the darkness and tell myself, 'You can do this.' But then I want to scream into the night, '*I can't, I won't, I shouldn't.*' But there is no choice.

I know enough about Usher to realise that this tunnel vision is closing in on me each day. That I might not be noticing it, but each second the view I have to look out of is getting smaller. That one day it will be like this . . . Blackness.

How will I cope? I think of people I've met through work, those who live in residential homes or with carers. At the moment, it's my job to be their advocate – but one day, might I be the one needing the care?

I try again to close my eyes, but it's no use.

I'm standing at the bus stop near my house. It's freezing cold – the type of cold that penetrates through your thick winter coat and buries itself deep inside your bones. My cheeks sting from the wind that whips around my neck like a scarf and finds any small gap to sneak under my collar and leave me shivering.

I'm angry, and the tears are pricking the backs of my eyes. It's 7 a.m. and still dark, and when a car splashes past I can see the silhouette of rain against its headlights. I'm thinking of the bunch of car keys that I passed on my way out of the kitchen this morning. I can still picture them there, on the edge of the worktop. I could cross the road, duck down one street and have them in my hand in five minutes. Just a few minutes after that I could be putting my key in the ignition, like I have done so many mornings, turning up the thermostat and switching on the fan heater, pulling out of my own road and past the rest of my fellow commuters here at the bus stop.

Except I can't. Not anymore.

But for a split second I think about it. And the fact that I can't just do it makes me furious.

This morning, I stood in the shower and mentally composed a text message. After I'd dried and wrapped myself in a white towelling bathrobe, I sent it to Mam, Julie, Alana and a couple of close friends.

It's been confirmed I do have Usher. I knew it. I'm going blind.

I'd pressed send. I don't know how long I sat there on the edge of the bed, waiting for a reply. Nothing came, though. I'm not sure what I was expecting. What was there to say, particularly over text? Unlike anyone else in that situation, I can't just pick up the phone and call people. I'm sure they wanted to ring me, to offer words of consolation or condolence, but they would have been lost on my ears.

It is the first time that I've shared my news with anyone, other than my partner. And that is the one thing stopping me from getting back in my car right now. I've told people I am blind. There is no going back. If I have an accident this morning, how will I ever forgive myself? I've been registered blind; it would be totally irresponsible to get into a car right now, even if nothing has changed in my sight from one day to the next.

So instead I stay shivering at the bus stop, biting back angry tears.

I stumble through the rest of the working week as if I'm jet-lagged. When people ask why I'm not driving to work, I make various excuses. I'm not ready to tell everyone the truth.

On Friday night, I head home to Gateshead on the train with all the presents I'd so carefully wrapped each evening. I'll spend the next few days having an early celebration with my parents, a time I wanted alone, before heading back to Sheffield in time for Christmas Eve. As the train pulls into the platform, I spot Mam's face, already scanning the crowd for mine. She looks so sad, so worried. This will be the first time we've been able to speak since I told her about the Usher. I can read every line on her face already; I know she's not going to be able to find the words.

If I could have protected her from this news, if I could have saved her from knowing I'd lose my sight, I would have done. Instead, I try to greet her with my cheeriest smile, my arms laden down with presents, but it doesn't fool her. We exchange a sympathetic sigh.

Just as I suspected, there are no words.

She tries to find some, though. 'You will be OK,' she says, and I see how much it pains her to say it, how difficult it is for her that she has to use these words to me, instead of telling me that it won't be Usher, like she has so many times before. But her eyes don't match the words that leave her lips, instead they're glazed with worry that I wish I could magic away.

'I know,' I try, perhaps equally as unconvincing.

I see the same look in Dad's eyes as we walk round to meet him in the car. 'Hello, pet,' he says, wrapping me in a hug as if I am a weary soldier, newly returned from the front-line. And right now, I feel it.

But as we make our way home, I'm just so glad to see them, to turn into my old street, to walk through the front door I know so well and feel nothing but wrapped in the love and comfort of my family.

And we do have a lovely weekend. Back home, I can forget that anything has changed in my life. I feel warm and loved.

By the end of the weekend, I feel refreshed and renewed. But back at the station, as Mam and I cross the concourse towards my train, I notice I'm walking a little more carefully than I might have done a week ago. And Mam is helping me a little more than she might have done ordinarily. After news such as I've just had, it's impossible for it not to change something.

'Take your time,' Mam says, cautiously. 'You don't want to fall.'

But suddenly Mam hears an announcement over the tannoy; she taps my arm so I look at her. 'Your train is about to leave!' she says. I look up at the screen and she's right. I'd got my times mixed up: my train isn't leaving at 15.49, it's 15.39 – in one minute.

I give her a quick kiss goodbye and then, grabbing the bags, I sprint across the bridge that separates the platforms. I run and run without looking back, without thinking, and make my train just in time.

When I sit down, there's a text message from Mam.

I can't believe you just did that, I'm still laughing, she writes. *The way you just sprinted across that bridge, you could be an ambassador for disabled people!* Xx

I'm giggling to myself now and I realise, as with so many things in life, that we'll get through this as a family by laughing.

Just like we always have.

Six months later, I celebrate my thirtieth birthday party. As I sit round a big table with all my friends, even surprise guests from Newcastle, for a moment I forget everything that's been happening over the last few months.

But if I'm honest, I've been doing that quite a lot recently. It's called denial.

So if people ask why I've given up my little green Ka, I tell them my eyes aren't as good as they used to be. I don't say I'm blind. I can't say it.

The months roll by, and on good days I make enquiries with

social services, I put my name down with guide dogs for the blind, I even enquire about the cane training. But that's on the good days, when I don't feel that my ever-decreasing tunnel is affecting me.

Every so often, I stand in front of the mirror in my familiar Breton striped top and count down to where I can see my fingers. Soon, there will be no more stripes to count down – my neckline is fast disappearing.

Diagram showing the field of vision that Jo has

I get on with life, with work, I pretend that the news I've been given doesn't exist. But increasingly, I am discovering more and more things that I have to cross off my list of things I can do, and slowly – very slowly at first – it is pulling me down.

I've always loved a run before work. For thirty minutes I'd pace the streets around my home, working up a sweat, and then dive into the shower back home. Whatever the weather, I'd be outside, feeling better for having had that run every morning. Yet recently I have been hurting myself more and more.

A few weeks ago I took a short cut home through the woods. As I ran, my breath keeping up with my fast pace, I couldn't possibly have seen where my feet were landing on the woody path. I tripped over a tree root and went flying. I landed on my front, the skin scuffed off my knees, a giant cut under my chin. I limped home, devastated, mentally crossing running off the list of things I could do.

Just the other day, I was in a bar getting a round of drinks in for my friends, but as I headed back to our table, I didn't notice the little table and stools in front of me. I walked straight into them, and the tray of drinks went flying, covering me and everyone around us in beers and gin and tonics. I scratched getting a round of drinks in off the list too, that independence lost to me.

I've got used to the shape of my lips apologising each time I knock a drink over on the table, or make some other error. And yet I refuse to tell people about my blindness, just carrying on the same as everyone else, when really it is obvious that there is a problem.

Perhaps people realise more than I notice; maybe they are just being polite. But it is hard for me not to note just how much I am hurting myself, just how unsafe my environment is now.

Even a gentle walk at the weekend ended up with me spraining my ankle. I'd gone out with some friends to a National Trust property. Crossing the green in front of the sprawling mansion, I hadn't spotted the little white stumps that keep the cars from driving onto the grass. Before I knew it, I was lying flat on my face, grass stains on my white jeans and my ankle throbbing with pain. I felt humiliated, embarrassed and helpless.

I am used to linking my arm through a friend's – I've spent my whole life doing it so that I can lip-read – but now I need them to guide me past obstacles, to lead me to a safer place to walk. I am having to give up my independence, I can't deny it for much longer.

And my GP has started to notice too.

'Have you thought about giving up work?' he suggests on one visit to repair yet another injury I've caused myself.

I stare at him blankly. There is no denying that I'm not coping physically, but mentally it hasn't occurred to me that I am anywhere close to losing my career.

I've coped with every change; my impending blindness hasn't meant that I've stopped working. I've just swapped my car for the train and carried on. And each thing that's happened, each injury I've caused myself through running or walking, I've adapted – or accepted I can't do it anymore.

But giving up everything I've ever worked for . . . That is not something I can accept so easily.

I remember how proud I'd been that first day at the House of Commons, how much I'd achieved in the north of England by representing disabled people, and their rights. Now my own disability was going to take away *my* right to work.

'Think about it,' my GP says.

But as I leave the surgery, there is something else weighing heavy inside me, a tiredness that I haven't acknowledged before.

Life has got harder, and it is getting increasingly more difficult for me to keep up. Yet I have managed to disguise it from my friends and even my family. The fact that I only go home to Gateshead a few times a year has made it easy only to put on some make-up and do my hair when I am due to see my family, so Mam and Dad have no idea just how hard I've taken my Usher diagnosis.

But alone at home, I am more comfortable in my jogging

bottoms. When I don't have to go out and face the world, I won't bother with any make-up. Sometimes even looking in the mirror pulls me down each morning, because I can see exactly what is disappearing from my view every day, every week, every month.

I might be managing to fool some people, but not myself.

There are times, though, during this great masquerade, when the reality of my situation cuts through. When I am carrying a hot coffee in a cafe and haven't noticed the toddler running along in my path. I sit down, shaken for a moment, to think about what might have happened if I'd tripped over her.

Life isn't just getting more dangerous for me, but for other people as well. And I realise I'd be irresponsible if I didn't acknowledge that.

Denial can only get you so far. Very soon, you reach a crossroads and then you and denial need to go your separate ways – or fall over the edge together.

Now is that time. I take my GP's advice a few weeks later and hand my notice in at work. Now here I am packing my desk into a small cardboard box, and I'm thinking back to all the jobs I've had over the years, which got me to this place now.

I think back to the hospital library, to my attempt to be a nurse, to Tedco and my disability awareness courses, and to all the strides forward I've made working for Radar.

I am just thirty-four years old. I still have so much to offer.

It doesn't seem fair. But I am tired of battling, too; tired of proving myself to people, to teachers, to the lecturer at Newcastle University who played such a cruel trick on me.

Perhaps, as it turns out, those people who didn't want me to sit at the front of the class as a child were right; perhaps I *didn't* have a right to work alongside everybody else.

But then: what was all that battling for? What was the point in all the bullying if it just left me in the same place I'd have been if I'd done nothing?

Right now, as I leave my office for the last time, I do wonder. But I also *want* to go home, to lay my head down and go to sleep, to stop battling if only for a while, and to give in to the deafblind person who I have become through no choice of my own.

My blackness is coming in thick and fast now, yet it isn't my eyes that are being covered but my heart. A depression that I've tried my whole life to keep at bay is starting to descend on me, and right at this moment, I am ready to lie down and let it cover me in its blanket of gloom, because I am so damn tired of trying.

Chapter Eleven

Even as I enter through the automatic doors, I know I don't belong here. Handrails line the walls, big yellow signs with thick black writing remind you where to go if you're lost, and every door is accompanied with bumpy Braille.

This is a residential home for blind people, and this could well be my future. I have an uneasy feeling in the pit of my stomach, the same one that has remained there since the day I was registered blind, and right now, standing in this wide corridor with ramps rather than stairs and a slightly sterile smell in the air, I'm more aware of it than ever.

Suddenly, I feel someone take my arm. I look round.

'This way, Jo.' The social worker smiles.

Even as I follow the group through to one of the kitchens, I know this place isn't for me. I'm more used to visiting residential homes like this for work, but now here I am on a 'taster group' session. My name has been on a list for this group for months, waiting patiently to be joined by others who have recently been given the same slip of paper as me.

They shuffle in alongside me, clearly with much less sight than my own eyes currently afford me. Many of them have sticks, some wear eye patches or dark glasses. As they take their seats at the front of the class, they look up and around aimlessly, totally oblivious to where the tutor is standing at the front of the room. The setting for our lecture is in one of the communal kitchens.

I feel more comfortable with the women who run the group than the other students who arrived here in the taxi with me today. As I left my front door and climbed in, it had reminded me of leaving Mam and Julie at home as a toddler, and being shipped off to another place I didn't want to be.

A man was sitting in the back beside me in the taxi; another lady in the front. If they were talking and I didn't answer, I hoped that I wasn't appearing rude. But neither of them seemed like they were in the mood to chat; perhaps like me they were coming to terms with the prospect of their new life too.

I'm now standing against the worktop in the kitchen, chatting to one of the tutors. I can see gadgets scattered around, ones I've been used to seeing at work.

Finally, there's a signal that the class is about to start, so I make my excuses to one of the social workers. As I prepare to walk away and rejoin the group of students, I see a look of confusion flash across her face: I don't think she realised I was with them.

I watch as the tutor starts to chat to everybody. Of course I don't hear any sound leave her lips, but I can see from her face how enthusiastic she is – though as her talk continues, I scratch that out in my mind and replace it with 'patronising'.

I glance at the group around me. Most people are staring off into the distance; very few of them are looking at the tutor. They look just like the people in the books and posters I was always so terrified to look at: they look helpless, lost.

There's that uneasy feeling in my tummy again. But the tutor clapping her hands and announcing that we're going to 'bake a cake!' snaps me out of my daydream.

We all get up and follow her into the kitchen. *I know how to bake a cake*, I think begrudgingly. *I'm blind; I don't need to be taught how to cook.*

Over in the kitchen, we gather round as she starts demonstrating some of the gadgets: there's an orange snail-type coil that hooks over the side of your cup to alert you when boiling water has reached the top; there's a sensor on the cooker to let you know when you're standing too close; and a kettle that beeps when it reaches boiling point.

But of course, I don't hear a thing. These items are lost on me.

I tentatively put my hand up. 'Are they making a noise?' I ask.

'Yes,' the tutor replies.

'But I'm deaf,' I tell them, and catch them sigh inwardly.

This taster group is not for me; how would I know when a cup of coffee has reached the top? What would be my warning if I was standing too close to the cooker as a deafblind person? I suddenly feel more out of place and more humiliated than ever.

I can see the social workers whispering to each other, double checking through their notes. One comes over and takes my arm.

'We didn't have anything in our files about you being deaf,' she says.

I sigh; I'd told two of them when I'd arrived.

'I think I'll just go home,' I tell them, and they agree to call me a taxi.

Waiting outside for the car to come, humiliated fears mingle with anger, that same fury that was bubbling up before, when I was at the hospital. I know from my own training courses that this is not the way to deal with people with disabilities, shunting us in and out like cattle, not having programmes that are tailor-made to suit someone's needs. How can a service dealing with the visually impaired not know about Usher?

I'd felt like I'd made such huge strides forward by signing up to this class, something I've avoided for a year, but as the taxi appears in the distance, I can't wait to get inside and have it drive me away from here.

I was right, I don't belong here – but it's not my fault, it's theirs.

Back at home over the next few days, I try to put that experience behind me, but it just feels to me like another reminder of the life that I've lost.

I'm sinking now, falling deeper and deeper into an unknown world, being pulled under by a current that I can't see or even feel. But like it or not, it's coming for me. Without the incentive to get ready for work every morning, I waste days at home now. At first it felt nice not feeling the vibration of my alarm clock under my pillow each morning, but those long lie-ins turned into midday showers, and more recently days spent in my jogging pants with hair that is well past its wash-by date.

So what do I do with my days? I have a little secret. Each morning, I take a box of photographs out of the cupboard, and I look at each and every one of them. I study each picture until I'm satisfied that it's burned an indelible image on my brain. There are photographs of Granddad on the beach, his bag stuffed with all our drinks and towels and changes of clothes, his bright grin, those twinkly blue eyes and the pink apples of his cheeks, just how I remember him as a child. My eyes scan every millimetre of the photograph for details I might miss: his seventies mustard shirt collar, the sand on his shoes, his brown corduroy jacket . . . but most of all that face I love and miss so much.

Next, I pick up a photograph of Mam in her twenties. Again I study every detail: those red flares, that purple T-shirt, her little waist – despite already being mam to Julie. Her blonde hair, and that smile she still wears today, the blue forget-me-nots in our backyard, the memories of hot sunny summers flooding back to me. I move onto the next picture.

On and on it goes. I lose hours and hours, days and days like this, but still I keep going through them. Pictures of me and Julie. The first ones of Alana in her terry towelling nappies, one giant safety pin securing the bundle in place, her chubby knees poking out the bottom, and rolls of baby fat that keep her warm. I test myself to see if I can close my eyes and still remember the way she toddled about the house – smiling if I do, panicking if I don't.

Can I still remember how Mam looks today with her long blonde bob, cute little fringe and lovely clothes, still stylish in her

sixties? The only lines she has on her face are those from laughing, and her smile is exactly the same as it was thirty years ago. Or
Dad, still the big tanned man he always was, but his hair is flecked
these days with more grey.

Julie might be in her late thirties now, but her grin hasn't
changed since the photos we had taken together as children,
complete with the gap in her teeth. And I study Alana's blue eyes
and her shoulder-length blonde hair, never a strand out of place.
She is always dressed in immaculate sporty clothes.

These memories, the ones that I'm so carefully imprinting on
my brain, will one day be all I have left. So I go on, picking one
photograph after another out of the box. If anyone pops round to
see me, I quickly tidy them away, but day after day I settle down to
my unending task, to look at every photograph I've ever taken so
as not to forget the faces of the people I love most.

It's all I've got left. What I see, the small amount of vision my
eyes still grant me each morning, is now what remains of my
window onto the world, and I am determined to make the most
of it.

I'm too embarrassed to tell anyone how I spend my days now.
They're only likely to tell me it might never happen, that I could
have decades of sight left still, but how do they know? How does
anyone know?

But as I stare at each picture, sometimes laughing at the memory
it conjures up, and sometimes crying, the emptiness inside me
isn't sated. The more pictures I pull out, the more I find. The
longer I spend staring at them, the more the images seem to elude
me. I can't keep up; there is a whole lifetime in some of these

boxes, and over the months I realise I don't have enough time to look at them all, to imprint all these onto my brain. There's not enough storage available.

And it's not just pictures of people that I'm desperate to keep inside, it's things too. My beloved Tyne Bridge, the curve of the arch, the criss-crossing of the steelwork, the green paint that looks so beautiful reflected in the river on a sunny blue-sky day.

I know even my view of this is disappearing. On journeys into the city on the train, I can't see as much of the arch as I used to. How can something so loved be disappearing in front of my eyes?

But I could say the same about any of the things I look at or the beautiful faces I just don't want to let go of. I never want not to be able to see Mam laugh. I want to see every one of those laughter lines on her face as she gets older. I can't imagine a day when I won't see the kindness in Dad's eyes, or the cheeky glint in Julie's and Alana's when they're up to something.

And the worst thing is, it's not just looking at them that I'll lose, it's talking to them too. Without me being able to lip-read, how will we even be able to tell each other how much we love one another? I know that my family will eventually adapt to a different communication skill like hands-on signing, but how can I compare that to sitting down and looking into their eyes?

My mind often runs away with me on these long days at home. My thoughts can be frenzied sometimes, racing away before I can keep up or calm them down.

These days I feel in such a panic to see everything I can, to make the most of every moment. I fill the house with fresh flowers and spend hours lost in the beauty of a bunch of daffodils or a few stems of orange gladioli.

When it comes time to visit Mam and Dad for the weekend, I'll dress myself up, doing my hair and make-up and fishing out some nice clothes from the back of the wardrobe. They have no idea of the way I waste my weeks at home, poring over photographs that I refuse to let my eyes let go of.

I feel myself falling deeper and deeper into a depression that is pulling me under, day by day, and one to which resistance is futile.

Perhaps it's a blessing in disguise when an appointment comes through for my cane training. Someone has already been round to measure me for a cane. I stood tall with my arms outstretched as the woman worked her way round all of my vital statistics like an expert seamstress.

'Hold out your arms,' she'd told me, before discussing which cane or adaptations I'd need.

On that day, I was still denying the fact that I needed one, so I waved my hand over any old basic white stick. The information she was sharing was irrelevant to me, I thought. This wasn't a choice that I was making; it was something being forced upon me.

But just like all the other things that are careering out of control right now, I know that resistance is futile.

Everything is black. The only 'sound' is my white noise. I feel completely alone, and frightened. I don't feel safe in this darkness; I need to be able to see. I need some light to feel safe.

Finally, I pull up my blindfold. 'I don't feel safe,' I tell my cane trainer.

'You are safe,' she promises me as I lip-read, one eye struggling to open fully thanks to the tight cotton wrapped around my head. 'Just try again.'

Trying to take her word for it, I pull the blindfold down again, feeling it tangle slightly in my blonde hair as I do. My right hand clutches the white cane, and I take one tentative step forward, swishing the cane just like I've been taught: *swipe to the right, back to the left, swipe to the right, back to the left.*

I take another step. I can feel the teacher's hand on my arm. I know what's ahead of me, a long straight corridor, and I try to hear her voice in my head, to picture her lips. *Let the cane do the work.*

But I can't do this; I don't feel safe without my eyes. All the time I'm trying to concentrate on moving forward, on letting the cane lead the path ahead – working its way around the objects that have been dotted along the floor, the giant ball on the end of the cane rolling its way around them, leading me the right way to avoid them – my mind is racing, and a tight knot of fear threatens to reach up from my belly and squeeze its hands round my neck.

Is this what it's going to be like for me one day? Is this how my life will be, plunged into a dark world, no light, no sound, just nothing?

'I'm sorry,' I say, pulling the blindfold up over my hair, light flooding into my pupils. 'I just can't do it.'

I need to see. I *need* to see.

I notice my teacher's shoulders slump. 'OK,' she says. 'We'll go back to practising without the blindfold.'

Up and down we go along the corridor in the University of

Sheffield. It's a dedicated part of the university that has been kept aside specifically for cane training the partially sighted or newly blind.

Just as my teacher had insisted, it is safe: just one long smooth polished path ahead of me. The only obstacles on the floor are those specifically put there for me to train with. And yet, as I go along without my blindfold, swishing the cane that's been specially made for me, the whole exercise feels pointless, because I can see.

It doesn't matter how many times the teacher tells me to let the cane do the work, I can't switch off my eyes because they're there, and they're working; even if they can't see what's underneath me, or to the side of me, all I need to do is look down.

So why am I here? Why do I need this?

Because of what is coming, a voice inside me says. *To be prepared.*

But it's not here yet, I answer back.

I finish the rest of the training but my heart isn't in it; instead my mind wanders as I go up and down the corridor a dozen more times. Which way does the bus go home? What will I have for tea tonight? Because I already want to be anywhere but here.

When we're finished, the teacher folds away the stick into a bag which I tuck under my arm. Back at home, I push it to the back of a cupboard and forget about it. As the weeks turn into months, there it sits.

Sometimes I go to that cupboard to fetch another box of photographs. I glance up at it, folded into five neat pieces, and I tell myself: *not yet*.

155

I don't show it to anyone; I don't want anyone to know I've got it. I can picture the look of horror on their faces, the way I'd look to them. I'd look blind. And yet I don't feel blind.

The other day I put my Breton striped top on and stood in front of the mirror. I can't see the neckline of my top anymore, only my own neck. The world is getting smaller in front of my eyes and yet I won't admit I'm blind because I don't want to lose my independence, I don't want to stop living the life I have, I don't want to admit I need help. I want to stay in control.

And then I remember: somebody once told me that being in control is knowing when to ask for help.

So the next time I go to the cupboard, I glance up at the cane, and this time I say: *soon*.

My arm jolts as I feel my cane hit against something hard. I look up, and can't help but do a little jig inside because, unlike the signposts back home in Sheffield, this one reads: Fifth Avenue.

It's my first time in New York and I've already fallen in love with the city. And – leaving aside the alluring appeal of the iconic hustle and bustle, the back-to-back traffic, the horns that irritate everyone else but are lost on my ears, the steam from the manhole covers, and the flashing *Don't Walk* signs – it is my cane which has played Cupid.

I'd decided when I was packing for this trip to reach for it at the back of the cupboard. Over the last few months I'd been feeling like I needed it more and more, but I wasn't keen to try it out on my home turf. So, instead, I'd decided to take it away to unfamiliar territory. Somewhere far away from home.

Immediately, the difference between Heathrow airport – where people and their carry-on suitcases darted in front of me, where my eyes were constantly spinning to make sure I didn't hurt myself or anyone else – and JFK airport was incredible. There, once I'd reached for my cane from my handbag, crowds parted to let me through, parents moved their toddlers out of my path, and officials collected me out of the line to allow me through without waiting.

Rather than my cane marking me out as different and inviting ridicule – as the phonic ear, the last symbol of my disability, had done – it in fact ensured I got VIP treatment.

As I'd left the airport with my cases and approached the taxi rank, the driver had sprung out of his car to help me. It was a revelation.

Everywhere I go here I am greeted with a smiling face, and not the pity I had so feared in people's eyes back home. Here, crowds part, people help me, and accept me, and life is so much easier.

And, more than anything, life is less stressful for me now. It took a bit of getting used to, but I remembered what my cane trainer had told me: *let the cane do the work*. So while my cane searches for obstacles on the ground, I look up and around this beautiful city. I marvel at the Flatiron Building, Times Square, the Rockefeller Center.

It is like being in a movie as I get used to the cane; even the sidewalk is more interesting because when my cane hits an unfamiliar obstacle, it's always something different to what we have back home: a fire hydrant or a *New York Post* kiosk. The ball on the end of my stick slowly rolls around it, giving me more time to explore, to look down, to soak up every detail from top to toe of the Big Apple.

It's like someone has lent me a film set to practise using my cane in, and that film set is New York. I'm convinced that if I look up, I might even spot Superman on top of one of the buildings, arms folded, cloak blowing in the wind, nodding down approvingly as I swish my stick this way and that along the streets.

And I walk for miles. Without the stress of watching out for hazards, walking has become enjoyable to me again.

It isn't just the sights, but the smells of New York: the mustard from the hotdog sellers who pop up on every corner; the perfume counters in Bloomingdale's. It is February and so cold that the air – heavy with the scents of the city – makes my eyes water as it circles my nostrils. I breathe in deep, snuggle cosily into my scarf and keep on walking.

Today I went to the Statue of Liberty, something I'd seen so many times on television and now was close enough to touch. It snowed while I watched her from the pier, thick snowflakes that seemed to fall as if in slow motion, the kind of snow that comes down in great clumps and lands on the end of your nose and is quickly wiped away before the cold seeps into your skin.

Everything about this city has been magical for me – and it turns out that its spell isn't broken when it's time to fly home. I return to the UK comfortable in my new-found status as a blind woman. I'd been in denial for such a long time, determined that I didn't need the cane, but I have realised while in the States that the cane *gives me back* my independence rather than robbing me of it. It isn't just an aid for me, it's a signal for other people to clear the path in front of me, to make life easier for me. And it's a huge turning point for me to realise this, but my work isn't over yet.

Back home at Heathrow, I don't hesitate to fish my cane out of my hand luggage, and I quickly realise that it isn't just in New York where people become more friendly, where people want to help you, as soon as they see your white cane, proudly displaying red stripes to let others know I'm also deaf.

When I finally get home, weary from travelling, my cane doesn't return to the back of the cupboard like a dirty secret. It sits proudly in my umbrella stand in my hallway.

My cane quickly becomes very precious to me after that trip: a prop that helps me to continue making my way around the world, sometimes with companions, sometimes on my own.

Of course, there are always going to be times when it catches me unawares – forgetting why people open a path for me in the street, for example, or the reaction on Julie's face when she first sees me with it. But the confidence that it gives me overpowers any flash of pity that I see cross anyone else's face, because I am OK – really, I am.

Chapter Twelve

With her blonde hair and long face, even I have to admit she looks a little like me. She walks into the living room with such a friendly vibe; one of those girls that you can't help but warm to. If she was human, the smile would be plastered all over her face – instead, her pink wet tongue hangs happily from slack jaws that reveal rows of white shiny new teeth.

Her name is Greta, she's eighteen months old and Guide Dogs for the Blind are sure that this dog is the perfect match for me. She is clever, calm, and possesses a glossy, sleek coat whilst all the time exuding a quiet confidence I know I can trust.

It hasn't been easy for me to get to the stage of accepting I need a guide dog. If I'm honest, none of this has been easy. There have been so many days when I've left the house automatically picking up my bunch of car keys, even though I haven't driven for years. There are other days when I leave to go out for the day without my cane. Being blind doesn't come naturally to me; it's something I have to remind myself of every day.

But then there are times when the reminders often come and tap me on the shoulder, before I've had chance to forget. Foreign beach holidays have become impossible for me now; I can't stand the hassle of trying to weave in and out of sunbeds around the pool, or trying to navigate the uneven Mediterranean paths that I so often longed to tread, but am now more likely to trip on.

Instead, I've resigned myself to holidays at home. I'll explore Devon, Cornwall, the Cotswolds – and for that, I tell myself, I need a furry friend. Over the last nine months, while I've been waiting for a guide dog, I've been trying to view it as a positive thing. I've never had a pet before, so that's how I try to look at it. My guide dog won't be so much of a prop as a friend who will open life up to me again, just as my inanimate cane has.

So that's how I've been seeing it, and that's why I'm so excited to meet Greta now.

One of the guide dog trainers, Ian, had come to interview me months ago. He'd looked around my house, asked about my interests, what I like to do – all for this moment of matching me with a dog that's perfect for me.

And here she is, Greta.

And, I must admit, she does put me instantly at ease about the whole thing.

When I'd first been handed those leaflets in hospital, the thought of having a guide dog had sent me into a spin. It had seemed to be the ultimate symbol of my new-found ultra-disabled status. If I closed my eyes and pictured a blind person, that's how

I saw them: white stick, guide dog, and no independence. I thought of someone like Paul, with whom I'd worked at Hunters Moor Hospital, and however much I tried to convince myself – and he had tried to convince me back in those days – that being blind was OK, I still couldn't embrace it.

Getting a guide dog was just another step towards embracing my blindness, and looking out from my tunnel and into Greta's deep brown eyes now, sitting here in my living room, her silent stare pleading with me to go out for a walk, I do feel some of my fears lifting a little.

'Shall we have a little walk out, then?' Ian says, slipping a harness onto Greta.

Her tail wags as we head for the door and I try to ignore the butterflies in my own tummy. This is all so new to me, how will I know what to do? I don't want to let Greta down. Luckily, we'll now have six weeks of training to equip me with the skills to let Greta know what I need her to do for me before she is handed over to me for good.

We're standing outside the house now and the trainer hands me the harness. It's hard and feels ugly and alien in my hand, a little like the cane had at first. But I tell myself: *you got used to that, you can get used to this too*.

Except I really don't know what to do, so we stand there, Greta and I, staring at each other, both of us no doubt sporting the same blank expression. I watch her furry eyebrows furrow. She looks ahead, a whole open path of tarmac awaiting her, except I'm stood stock still. I don't know what to do.

I search the trainer's face for some idea. 'Let's go,' I lip-read, and we start walking, but as we do, something doesn't feel quite right. Am I holding the harness too tight, or too loose? How do I know which way to lead her – or does she lead me? The harness feels awkward in my hand. Greta hesitates, jerks, pauses. I try not to trip as I go forward when she hasn't had the signal from me to go. Our collective feet stumble, making for one awkward moment after another.

I look to the trainer for assurance, not realising that he's been trying to tell me what to do the whole time we've been walking. But of course his instructions are lost on me: I can't hear him.

I have to stop to look at him; Greta willingly obliges.

'Hold the harness like this,' he says, adjusting my hands. We walk a few steps again, and then we need to stop again for me to check something else.

Greta stops and starts, stops and starts, so patiently, but it's clear to both me and the trainer in an instant that this isn't going to work.

I can't lead Greta confidently because I don't know what I'm doing, and she is quickly losing patience and interest. I don't know what to do because I can't hear the trainer's instructions as we walk along. Instead I'm looking at the path ahead of me, at her silky caramel coat, her wagging tail. My nerves aren't helping much either.

I see her ears twitch, confused. She knows it's not working too.

It's impossible for the trainer to guide me when all of his advice escapes my ears. And in the meantime, Greta is getting confused with all the stopping and starting.

We persevere, but after a couple of hours it's obvious that it won't work.

As we head back home, and the trainer takes the harness, I watch how Greta trots along without hesitation and my heart feels heavy in my chest. I'd been so excited about Greta, but I'm just not ready for her.

Back in my living room, we decide I'll need to take a prop out at first, to learn the ropes with a 'fake' dog, before I get my hands on a real one again. But, sadly, Greta can't wait for me; she has to go off to another owner. Her brown eyes look sad as the trainer leads her out of my living room; she hesitates, her tail drooping slightly, and looks back at me as I wave her goodbye.

I watch from the living room window as the trainer pops Greta into the back of his car. I feel like I've let her down, that actually she is the right dog for me, but I'm just not the right owner for her.

I'm trying to adapt to life as a blind person, but this time it's my lack of hearing that's been the problem. I feel right back where I was as a child, unable to keep up with what others around me are doing, and now because of my deafness, Greta has had to go to someone else.

'There'll be another dog along very soon,' the trainer told me reassuringly before he left. I'm sure he's right, but I felt an affinity with Greta.

Will I ever have my perfect match again?

We must look like a right pair walking down the street, the guide dog trainer and me. After all, I'm clutching a harness with an invisible dog on the end. Picture those props that comedians use in sketches when they're walking a fake dog: the long, stiff lead, a circular collar on the end but . . . no dog.

And that's what I'm doing now, pacing the streets with Ian and my invisible dog. I see a driver in a car do a double take; people on buses that go by stare out the window and point. We must look ridiculous, so I can see why.

I had felt a bit sad when Ian returned without Greta a few weeks after that disastrous first walk. It didn't matter how much he assured me that she'd gone to a nice new home, I still felt like I'd let her down, and the whole experience had knocked my confidence a bit.

Of course, Guide Dogs for the Blind are used to training deaf-blind people, but somehow – perhaps in the excitement of finding Greta for me – it hadn't worked out for me.

But I've been training with my invisible dog for a few weeks now, and all the instructions are starting to make sense.

Rather than finding the process hard, I've been trying to see the humour in my long walks with an invisible dog. Often I'll reach down and pat it while the trainer and I laugh. I'll remind it to sit when we come to a crossing in the road, or call 'walkies!' as we leave the house.

But there is also a lot to learn. What many people might not realise is the exact job of a guide dog. Just like the cane, you do have to learn to let the dog do the work, but they need guidance from you too, they're still an animal, so anyone with a guide dog needs to have some kind of sight, however slight.

The way they are, though, is simple: as the name implies, they are your guide. For example, for me, my tunnel vision means that anything beneath me is a mystery, unless, of course, I look down. But the guide dog is my eyes on the floor. If there is a bin there, he will walk round it, not because he's taking me so much as he doesn't want to walk straight into something and hurt himself.

And that's how it works. If there's a bin in the way, I'll feel the harness guiding me round it. If we're crossing a road, he doesn't want to get himself run over so he'll wait on the path until it's safe to cross.

And he's also a signal to other people that I need them to move out of the way.

But he needs guidance too, subtle signals that tell him which way to go. I learn over the weeks with my invisible dog how to do a little left or right gesture with my finger above the dog's head as I hold the harness. The dogs have been trained before they are partnered up to respond to these signals – that's why Greta didn't know what to do because *I* wasn't guiding *her*.

And that's what I've been learning: how to hold the harness, how to relax my arm, how the dog sits at a crossing until you both realise it's safe to cross.

And now I feel confident and ready for a real dog instead of my invisible one. I want to bury my hand into real fur, come home to that comforting smell of a dog basket, see those brown eyes looking up to me for reassurance, throw a ball and watch a dog tear across fields just like I would have done a few years before. I want all the fun of having a little canine friend.

The following day, Ian texts me with some exciting news.

We've got a dog for you. His name is Vance. He's a flat-coated retriever. I'll bring him round later.

I look up at my sister Julie, with whom I'm having lunch, and show her the text.

'Vance?' she says, wrinkling her nose slightly.

'Vance,' I repeat. It seems an odd name. But while I say it over and over, getting used to the way it rolls off my tongue, I feel something else swelling in my tummy – excitement. The moment is finally here: I'm going to meet my new doggie pal.

That afternoon, I watch the clock and my tummy twists and turns as I wait for them. And then, through the window, I spot them. The car pulls up, the trainer gets out and out jumps Vance. He bounces alongside Ian as they walk towards the front door. As soon as I open it, in he bounds.

With his silky black coat that curls and waves at the end, he looks more like a girl. He has a long serious face like Greta . . . and that's where the similarity ends, because while she had exuded a quiet calmness, there's nothing like that with Vance. He's like the guy who turns up to the party clinking with bottles of wine; he's here for the fun more than for the job. He wags his tail over and over, fanning anyone who comes near him. His pink tongue hangs happily out of the side of his jaw and I notice it has a little brown birthmark on it that makes it look like he's been eating mud.

I instantly take to him; you can't not. We go out for a walk and it's completely different to that first time with Greta, thanks to my training – and his. There's no hesitation: he bounces along happily in front of me, wagging his tail, smiling at passers-by. People are watching us and Vance loves it.

By the time we've been round the block and back, I'm absolutely, upside down, inside out, in love with Vance. His energy, his happiness, his lust for life means he is definitely the one for me.

When Ian leaves with him a couple of hours later, the house already feels empty without him. Ian will bring him back each day for more practice over the next six weeks, until we're confident to be left alone.

Each day after that, I'm up and out each morning, waiting for Vance to arrive. As the days roll on, he greets me more as a friend, and every day the harness feels more and more natural in my hand.

I can see how Vance will help me now, how he will change my life. I'll have that extra bit of confidence going out, just like the cane has given me, but this time I'll have a companion, too.

As our training continues, having a guide dog proves every bit as liberating as I'd anticipated. With Vance by my side, I now have the confidence to walk along the street having a conversation with a friend; I can lip-read again because my furry friend is keeping an eye on the floor while I chat.

And it's not just friends I can talk to either. I notice how kids run over to pat the dog, how I then stand chatting to their mums as they fuss over him.

Vance has opened up a whole new world to me, a world filled with people and chat and life; he's broken down barriers that the cane had perhaps put up. I think back to how frightened I was by the leaflet the hospital gave me telling me to contact Guide Dogs for the Blind, and I wonder why I ever worried.

Today, as we near the end of our training, Ian suggests we go for a drink in the local coffee shop. Quite confidently, I lead the way with Vance.

It's only as we approach the coffee shop that I spot someone I haven't noticed before in the window. She is about thirty-five, dressed like me: a grungy look with tight jeans and a faded T-shirt. She's wearing the same light thin scarf wrapped around her neck, which is adorned with beaded necklaces; she's wearing baggy tassled boots just like mine. She looks cool, except for one thing: she has a harness in her hand and on the end of it is a guide dog, a dog that looks exactly like Vance.

I stop briefly and glance at Ian, who I realise is talking to me, but my attention is pulled back to that woman – that blind woman. And then I realise: it's the reflection in the coffee shop window; it's me.

It's the first time I've seen myself as a blind woman, and it feels like being punched in the stomach.

Ian is asking me what I'd like to drink and somehow I manage to order a coffee. But while my mouth might be saying the words, my mind is spinning back years to Paul, who I worked with at the library: a blind man and his guide dog. And now it's picturing the blind people in the books and posters who had frightened me so much when I thought I was losing my sight. It's *that* image, *that* disabled woman. I've been training for weeks now but somehow, with the excitement of getting Vance, I hadn't realised: I have become her.

I manage to sit through the coffee with Ian, we chat and laugh, but inside this fear, this feeling, is turning and twisting and chok-ing me like ivy reaching up from my gut.

I want to get home, I want to get away, from here, from Ian, from this dog.

From my life.

That night, at home, I lock myself away in the bathroom. I fill the room with steam and sink into my hot bath and then I cry. Hot tears that spill into the water, over and over they pour down my cheeks and into the bubbles below. I cry for everything I've lost, I cry for the eyes I haven't yet let go of, I cry for the world that is getting smaller each and every single day.

I cry for the girl who danced at discos until her feet were numb, for the woman who ran across the bridge at Newcastle Station for her train. I cry for everything I've lost and everything I haven't – yet – but that I'm still not ready to say goodbye to.

I cry for the woman who left the hospital staring at that bunch of leaflets in her hand saying she was blind.

I cry for all the hours I spent staring at photographs to burn them into my brain, and how, even now, I catch myself staring at Mam, trying to recreate the colour of her eyes over and over whenever I close my own.

I cry and cry and cry for myself. For the woman who isn't ready to turn out the light, who wants to keep looking out and yet doesn't have any choice.

I cry for the old Joanne. And I think: *why me?*

And then I must stop, and just stare, because I'm not sure how much time has passed, but the water is icy cold and when I move again it makes me shiver. Even my wet hair has dried in the shape that I was lying on it. And I realise that this is the lowest I have ever been, sitting here in this ice-cold bath.

I get out and hastily dry myself, slipping into my pyjamas and between the sheets of my bed.

I fall into a deep, exhausted sleep that night. I am getting used to the blindness, I realise that. But just like everything else, it needs to be one day at a time.

I'm sitting on a park bench eating a sandwich. It's the beginning of autumn and piles of leaves are scattered on the ground. The hazy sunshine cuts through the crisp air and warms my back as I sit looking out over the park. Every so often I look up from my food to scan the field for Vance. It's nice to bring him out to be a real dog as often as I can, to let him off the lead and see him run until he looks so tiny in my eyeline, a little black speck in the distance. He'll come back eventually, his pink tongue hanging happily from his mouth and his hot breath making steam in the cold air before his wet nose.

Every dog, and especially guide dogs, deserves to feel the wind in their furry ears, to run so far that they feel free from the lead, to be without the harness for a few moments, to have an hour off and just be a dog.

But suddenly, as I look up, I notice there seems to be some kind of commotion. People have stopped to stare, others are pointing, a few are sniggering into their hands, and then there's the odd one who is scanning the rest of the field, clearly looking for someone, and instantly my heart sinks and I know who: me.

My tunnel follows their gaze and soon discovers the draw of such attention: Vance. And what is he doing? What he always does when I bring him out and set him free: he's humping another dog on the path. On and on he goes, not put off by its shape or size, or indeed whether the dog's owner is trying to get it away.

His tongue hangs from his mouth, his eyes are set in a

determined smile, and as usual I throw down my sandwich and bound over to drag him away.

'Vance!' I shout, and it's only when he sees me that he snaps out of whatever trance he's got himself into. And then he runs, further and further away, as I stand apologising in the middle of the field.

Everything is a game to Vance, I've learnt over the last year. It was one of the things that drew me to him initially, but – as with a lover you've long since fallen out of lust with – I've become tired now of trying to keep up with his next naughty antic.

When we leave the house in the morning to get to an appointment, he pulls me towards the park. If we're sitting having coffee with a friend he'll be humping the cushion, the chair, my friend's leg . . .

If I give in and we go to the park, I'll wait for ages for him to come back. I've tried bribing him with treats, and I thought it worked for a while, but these days he'll just gallop over to me to get them, and then in one split and cheeky second he'll snatch it from my hand and bound back over the other side of the field. I've tried leaving the park, hoping he'll panic without me . . . but he just runs off the other way.

And there are other things, too – like the fact he sees himself as more human than me. When I get on the bus I'll let him into the seats first to get settled on the floor. But when I sit down myself and glance out the window, there he is, sitting alongside me. Nose to nose we sit there, him watching the people go by outside, and me chastising him to get down.

Not that he pays any attention.

If you saw it from the street, a bus going by with one extra furry passenger, it might look amusing. And even I have to admit it is. Vance is so happy, so cheeky, such a joker, that it is hard to get mad at him.

But he's also a working dog, and he's not making my life any easier. In fact, I hate to say it but he's making it worse.

At home he is great fun if we want to play ball. We have a game called 'Find it', where we hide his favourite toy somewhere in the room while he waits in the hallway, and he bounds in searching for it – never failing to return it to me.

But going out with Vance is a nightmare. I want to turn left, but he is determined to go right to the park. If I could take him for the company and the cane for the help, I would. But I can't.

I wait in the park that day for Vance to come back, his eyes alive and sparkling, and then I finally get him back on his lead. 'Bad dog!' I say, vowing to myself that when I'm home I'll have to call Ian. But as we walk back in the autumn sunshine, even I can't hide the smile that creeps across my face. Vance might be naughty, but he's funny, too.

A few days later, Ian arrives, and he's not happy. He takes Vance out on the harness to see if he behaves with him. Perhaps he's thinking a firmer hand might work. But, as we reach the pedestrian crossing, Vance refuses to cross – he knows the park is the opposite way. Ian pulls on the harness, but that furry bottom won't budge.

I bite my lip as I stifle a giggle. I can't help it. Ian looks red and flustered, and all I can do is shake my head.

He takes Vance away for a few weeks of top-up training, but it's no good. He isn't suited to guiding; he's not the dog for me. They soon find him another job, as an airport sniffer dog. I keep in touch with the people he went to. I would have loved to have kept Vance myself, he was always the same happy character who bounded into my house that very first day, ready for a party. He was fun-loving, friendly . . . but just far too naughty.

I didn't find it hard being without a dog once Vance had gone – after all, he'd been great company but he hadn't really *helped* – but six months later I find myself staring out of my window as I watch another dog jumping out of the car parked outside my house.

This one has a sleek black Labrador coat, a full face and a sturdy body. His tail is wagging as he walks through the front door and into my living room, picking up the black Labrador puppy doorstop on the way. As the door shuts behind him, he plonks himself down in the middle of the carpet and snuggles up to the stuffed toy.

'Do you like him?' Ian asks me. And as he says it, Matt gets up from the floor, pads over to me and puts his face in my lap. Then he looks up at me with those chestnut brown eyes, eyebrows raised in expectation, and I know: he's the one.

From the first day I start the training with Matt I feel content. We walk out on a sunny afternoon and I look down happily at the shadow the pair of us cast on the path in front of me. With his sweet little ears bouncing up and down as we walk, and his tongue hanging joyously from his mouth, he looks so cute – like a caricature of a typical Labrador.

I instantly feel safe with Matt. Being with him reminds me of the days when I used to walk to the bus stop with Granddad, putting my tiny hand into his big one.

Over the weeks, I get to know Matt better. He's full of life, he has a brilliant energy, but he knows first and foremost that he has a job to do. He's strong and sturdy, he loves going to new places and meeting new people. He doesn't turn right for the park, he turns left – just in case we're going on an even better adventure.

At home he makes the perfect companion. If I sit reading in the evening he'll be there too, lying on my feet, using my slippers as a pillow. As long as he's next to me he's happy, and I feel the same about him. Often, as he naps, I'll feel him twitch and look down to see him having a horrible dream; I'll gently prod him with my feet to wake him from it.

When people come to visit, particularly children, he'll leap about and spin round and round on the driveway. I laugh because, really, he's only doing what I wish I could do.

And that's how he is, he loves life – and I can see he wants me to love it too. So ever so slightly, one day at a time, I feel myself thawing.

I start to let go and look to a future, even if I can't see it. And I don't know it yet, but it's going to be Matt who'll encourage me to pick up that harness and start enjoying the journey again.

Chapter Thirteen

Imagine someone passing you the most beautiful flower and you not being able to look at it. Or seeing a smile on a child's face and not being able to greet it with a similar one on your own. Imagine seeing something as beautiful as the seaside on a sunny day and, instead of seeing the beauty, you simply resent it for existing in the first place. Or staring at your someone you love *while you still can* but not feeling any joy in that, just sadness of what might be.

That is how I've lived my life for the last few years since I was registered blind. I'd stopped seeing the beauty in life – because what was the point when it was fast disappearing in front of me?

When I look in the mirror now, there is no point in counting the stripes on my Breton top, because it has disappeared altogether. Instead, all I can see is a glimpse of my chin, nothing else around the outside.

As I'd lived my life – or, should I say, existed – in the last few years, my view on that life had been getting smaller and smaller; and not just the physical view, but the mental one, too. As, one by one by one, I'd crossed things off my list of things that I couldn't do anymore, the world shrank, bit by bit. I couldn't run, I couldn't get up and buy a round of drinks from a bar, I couldn't drive, I couldn't go for long country walks. And not only had all of these things been taken away from me, but I also faced years ahead of more and more of my favourite things being stolen from me, like conversations with people I loved, or seeing my mam's smile.

One day, I would no longer be able to appreciate the beauty in the world around me, so what I'd decided in the last few years was that I might as well stop looking, even while I can. Why have the pleasure of seeing things that would soon be robbed from me anyway?

I suppose, in some twisted logic in my mind, I'd thought that if I stopped looking at all these beautiful things, it might not hurt as much when they were taken from me. To make yourself fully blind before your time might seem an odd thing to do, but for me it had become a way of life. If I was going to lose my sight, I might as well start doing it sooner rather than later, closing my eyes to life before they were closed without my say-so.

Slowly, each day, anger had bitten off another piece of me, and I'd become bitter. And that's how I'd lived the last four years since it was confirmed I had a retinal disease.

Except now I am here, on top of a hill in the middle of the Peak District – and it is like someone has just opened my eyes.

The sun is going down and the sky has turned pink, and there is that wondrous feeling of spring in the air: the lighter evenings that tend to be bathed in sun a little bit longer, that feeling of hope in the air when you see buds breaking into flowers on trees and fresh green leaves uncurling from their branches. The snowdrops start to droop to make way for bright new daffodils and tulips springing up in their path, and life has returned to all of us as we shake off the coldness of winter.

As I stand on this hilltop, Matt is running round me, his ears flapping in the wind and a wide smile plastered all across his furry jaw, and I know exactly how he feels – because for the first time in four years I feel it too. There is a really beautiful view in front of me, here, today, now, and I have just realised for the first time how silly I am to waste precious time by not looking at it.

Life is suddenly beautiful again. Why close my eyes off to the glory of the sun when it's still there like a constant, rising and setting every day? Why refuse to look at the flowers when they make such an effort to showcase their beauty, year in, year out?

And it's Matt who I have to thank for opening my eyes again.

He doesn't pad alongside me when I take him off the lead, he gallops like a greyhound, running back to me every so often as if to say, 'Come on, here's how you do it, watch me!' His nature sees the best in everything – such as the pleasure of tearing across an open field – and he has reminded me to do the same.

It was Matt who gave me the confidence to start walking in the countryside again. Getting away from the hustle and bustle, and with all that wide open space in front of me, I started to realise just how big the world is. Yes, my view of it might be smaller than it was, but as my tunnel got narrower, the world around me got bigger.

And as I stand here now, looking out at that whole world in front, beneath and above me, I realise there are so many ways to see beauty.

I don't think anyone has realised just how much I've struggled these last few years. I've put on a brave face, tried to show them that I was positive when they saw me with a stick or a guide dog, but every single day has been painful as I waited for the blackness to descend. And that is what I was waiting for: darkness, nothing.

And yet, four years have gone by and I'm still here, looking out on the world, even if it is from a smaller perspective.

Finally facing my blindness meant, at last, that I was more inclined to find out more about Usher. That was an eye-opener in itself – because the darkness at the end of the tunnel that I thought awaited me was not there at all. Yes, there was a tunnel . . . but there was always going to be some light at the end of it, I learnt. People with Usher may not lose all of their vision: the tunnel gets smaller, but what about the bit you *can* see? In my blindness, I'd forgotten about that. It might only be something tiny, but it was *something*.

And standing up here now I realise that I can keep looking. That as long as there isn't nothing, there is beauty to drink up, to scoff down, to wallow and dance in.

That moment up there in the Peak District is the moment I decide to change my life. I'd gone up that hill a blind woman, but I come down a seeing one; not so much in my eyes, but in my heart.

There is still a world out there, and I decide there and then,

JO MILNE

somewhere in the middle of the Peak District, that I am going to live in it.

One of the first things I do over the next few weeks is decide to get a tattoo. I realise that I've allowed life to pass me by these last few years and I want a permanent reminder to grab every moment of it, whatever my life might look like. So I have the ink indelibly printed on the back of my forearm, so I can look at it if ever I close my eyes again. A Bob Marley quote: 'Love the life you live, live the life you love.'

For me, it is an acceptance of my disabilities. It is wrapping the blindness and the deafness up into one huge group hug and saying: 'It's OK, we can take it from here, together.'

I'm not pushing my disabilities away anymore. I'm not that twelve-year-old girl who didn't want to wear hearing aids because she wanted to fit in with all her classmates. I'm not the woman who refused to get the cane down from the back of the cupboard. I am me, Joanne Milne, a deafblind woman who, just like so many of us, is just trying to do her best with the cards that life has dealt her.

But something else is stirring inside me too – a feeling that I can do better, that even though I've embraced the life I am living now, I could live an even better one.

And I have an idea how . . .

There has always been, in the back of my mind, the knowledge that life might be different for me. I'd worked enough over the years with people with all sorts of disabilities to know that there are so many options out there for them.

And there were for me too, but it has taken me until my late thirties to ask about them.

Perhaps I was afraid, perhaps my own disability was as much a part of my person as the nose on my face, but whatever had happened to me up there on a hilltop in a split second has changed the way I view myself.

And that's why I'm here now, back in a hospital waiting room, waiting for a nurse to tap me on the shoulder and lead me into the consultant's office.

I glance up at the door and wonder what awaits me behind it. This waiting room is like many others I've been in before; the sage green walls and vinyl floor tiles. In one corner there is a basket of toys and books for kids. I picture two-year-old me toddling over to play with them as Mam watches on.

But Mam isn't here with me today; this is something I want to do on my own. There is a feeling of nervous expectation in my tummy, beyond that I'm not sure whether to feel excited or frightened. So my insides hold on tight to the knot, hanging on, waiting for an answer. And then the door opens.

The nurse ushers me in to meet Mr Coulson.

'Your GP has referred you to me because you'd like to know more about cochlea implants,' he says. 'What do you hope we can do here for you today?'

I'd always known that cochlea implants were possible, ever since I was a child, but I'd never met anyone who'd had them. What I did know, though, was that they could make deaf people hear for the first time. I just didn't know if they could work for me. And to be honest, before now, I didn't really care. I was confident about being deaf, I was fine the way I was, and I didn't feel the need to be anything else – until I'd started to lose another sense. Then I knew that life could be better for me.

The surgery itself is complicated; in fact, it's classed as brain surgery.

A cochlea implant does the job of the inner ear, converting sound into electrical signals that the brain can convert back into sound. The user wears a hearing aid round the back of the ear, which is connected magnetically to the implant inside the brain, which sends the signals to the auditory nerve. Twenty-two electrodes are weaved on a wire into the existing cochlea, and the brain converts the signals it receives from them into sound.

Nothing is possible without some kind of activity from the auditory nerve; if that's not working there's nothing for the implant to work from. But with even the smallest percentage of activity, you have something – the possibility.

What amazes me, though, is that Mr Coulson can't believe I haven't been referred to him before. But then, my condition hasn't been all that familiar to my medical team. There have been so many times that I've sat in my GP's surgery while he's googled Usher. Most of the research I've done myself, poring over endless leaflets and web pages to find out more about my condition.

But here, Mr Coulson doesn't need to be told. He takes a quick glance through my records and then looks up at me.

'It could work incredibly well for you,' he smiles. 'I think you're an ideal candidate for a cochlea implant.'

The knot in my stomach takes a while to undo, and the

information takes a while to sink in, but finally, my brain pieces it together. The man sitting opposite from me, the man with the huge smile plastered from cheek to cheek, is telling me that he can make me hear, that he can turn a deaf girl into a hearing one. I've come here with the hope of having one ear done; he's saying why not two, why not experience hearing utterly and completely?

In my mind, a cochlea implant has always meant more powerful hearing aids. It would be turning up an internal volume on my white noise; there will still be muffled sound, but just more of it.

'I've always wished I could turn up the volume,' I tell him.

But the way Mr Coulson is talking now, gesticulating with his hands, smiling as he describes it, he is talking about a new woman, a hearing one who doesn't understand just what a precious gift he may be able to bestow on her.

He shows me what the implants look like, showing me the two pieces that hook around the top of the ear, much like my hearing aid, and then the magnet that sticks to the side of the head, communicating with the implant inside. When he places them back down on the desk, I notice they make a love heart shape when they're joined together.

As Mr Coulson talks, he explains the wonder that could await me. He describes a world where I could chat to friends around the table, speak on the phone, watch TV and *hear* music – but there are risks too. If the auditory nerve is damaged during the op, it will strip me of even the white noise I've come to rely on. I would be plunged into the kind of silence I have at night when I place my hearing aids on the bedside table.

'After all,' he says, 'any surgery carries a risk. There is no guarantee that it will work.'

But it's the way he talks, the positivity that radiates from him, that makes me convinced that taking that risk might be a small price to pay, that actually it's minimal, that the rewards might well far outweigh anything that might go wrong.

I leave the Queen Elizabeth Hospital in Birmingham, where the specialist is based, full of hope and joy. I might be losing my eyes – but is there really a chance that Mr Coulson is going to give me back my ears in exchange? My tummy does a little dance as I glance out of the window of my train back home. I imagine what life might be like if I could hear. I picture something as simple as going for a walk with Matt and all the sound colouring in that routine thing we've done time and time again; hearing the happy chuckles of children as they spin round and round on the roundabout, the different noises of animals that greet me across the fence whenever I take Matt for a walk in the countryside – I've often wondered what noise the geese are making when they waddle over to me, their orange beaks going up and down. I look up at the blue sky and wonder what sounds I'm missing up there: planes flying through the skies, leaves shaking on tree branches, birds gliding above me – do all these things make sounds, or are they silent?

There is a whole world out there and Mr Coulson is offering me the chance to be part of it.

Over the next few days and weeks, I share my news with friends and family, but while they're happy, they treat the idea of an operation with some trepidation – particularly Mam. 'But you're OK as you are,' she says; she's worried about the risks.

I can understand that. Everyone has seen how capable I am, how well I cope with life, how I get on with things. How I've tackled my deafness *and* now my blindness. I can see how they think I am fine the way I am, but there's another part of me that wants to say: don't you think I deserve to have better? Don't you think I want to know what it's like to hear sound, to know what your voice sounds like, to lie back and hear my own breath, to open up a whole new world?

They are generally positive, but even if I can't hear the fear in their voices, I can see it in their eyes.

'What if it goes wrong?' Mam says.

But what if it doesn't? What if there's a chance that I'll take my old hearing aids out one last time and never ever put them back in again, and instead let my ears do the work that they were created to? To hear, to listen. Just imagine.

It has been a painful realisation over the last few years that there are things I once loved to do that I can't do anymore. I have had to accept that my disability won't allow me to run like I used to, or to socialise like I did in my twenties or to zip across the country in my little green car.

And I've found this loss of all the things I loved and held dear paralysing. Yet I'm now committed to looking at things completely differently. Rather than thinking I can't do something, I'm now determined, instead, just to find a new way.

The depression that I'd felt weigh so heavily on me for the last few years has lifted, but I think I know of a way that I can make it disappear once and for all. And that's why I find myself here, now, my hands twisting awkwardly in my lap, my fingers unable to keep still. Every so often I wipe my palms on my new tweed trouser suit that I've bought especially for today, but seconds later my nerves see to it that they're clammy again.

It's been a long journey to get here; a journey full of different changes to my life. Today is just the latest step along my new road.

Not long ago, I'd realised that not being able to exercise had only exacerbated the negative feelings I'd had inside. I knew I had to run again. And while I might not be able to pound the streets where I lived for fear of tripping over on uneven pavements or indeed people, there was another way.

I joined a gym, and there, on the treadmill, I could run for hours. It must have looked strange to the other people there, watching the blind woman with a white stick negotiate the exercise bikes and rowing machines to find her way to the treadmill, but once I got on it, felt the energy coursing round my body, my legs working harder and harder to keep up with the belt, the sweat pouring off my chest, there was no stopping me.

And that's how I decided to tackle other things too. It had been so painful giving up my car, but I started to see the pleasure in taking train journeys. I'd buy a nice coffee and a magazine and sit and look out of the window at the view. I made the experience more than just getting from A to B.

And when it came to socialising with friends, yes, it was hard that I couldn't go to the bar anymore, or order coffees and carry them back to our seats for fear of tripping on a toddler and sending the whole lot flying. But instead I convinced myself to enjoy being able to sit back and relax, to take pleasure in being waited on.

Life went from monochrome to Technicolor overnight, and yet nothing had changed apart from my attitude.

And I'm going to need every inch of my new positive attitude to get me through today. I wipe my sweaty palms on my trouser legs once more.

Suddenly, the door opens and I'm called through. I swallow hard and stand up, my stride appearing far more confident than I am on the inside.

Why? Because this is a job interview, my first in years, and I'm determined that this position is perfect for me.

The role is to be an Usher Mentor Coordinator for the deaf-blind charity, Sense. It means I'd be working as a mentor and recruiting other mentors to work with people who have the same condition as me. I'd be reaching out to people who might still be in the same depths of depression that I'd been in for the last four years, who might not realise there is a life after they've been diagnosed, people who need to be reminded that there literally is still light at the end of that tunnel. And everything that I've been through, the journey that I've been on has – I believe – brought me to this point so that I can help others.

I sit down in the chair in front of a panel of four people. None of them is deaf or blind, but they all want to know about me.

I tell them about my work for Radar fighting for the rights of disabled people, and I tell them about my own experiences of Usher. They ask me question after question and I answer them clearly and confidently, even though inside my heart is racing.

I'd first seen the job advertised on the Sense website a couple of months before. It had seemed perfect from the start, apart from one thing – it was based in Surrey, miles from my home in Sheffield. I'd decided not to go for it.

But six weeks later, the advert reappeared, and I took that as a sign. I quickly sent off my application – and here I am now.

'Thanks very much for your time, we'll be in touch,' one of the interviewers says half an hour later as I'm shown to the door.

As I leave their offices, I glance at some of the other people working away inside. How I long to be a part of their world again . . .

Two weeks later, as I struggle into the house with my supermarket shopping, there on the doormat is a letter from Sense. I rip it open and hold my breath.

We're delighted to offer you the position . . .

I've done it.

A few weeks later, I make up a packed lunch and Matt and I head out to the office for the first time. I'd negotiated with them to work from their Wakefield office rather than their Surrey branch.

There are perhaps some people who wonder why I felt the need to go back to work when I could have had a comfortable life at home, but I simply felt like I had so much more to give.

I am thirty-eight, and I've only just remembered: the world out there has much, much more to offer me yet . . .

ahead again, buoyant with energy that will see us both through the day.

By the time I reach my office, everyone already knows we're there; they tell me that they heard Matt's paws padding up the stairs, the excited pant of his breath, signalling our arrival.

My colleagues are lovely, chatty and friendly. But what I've enjoyed the most is getting out and meeting people, others who have Usher just like me.

I've learnt so much about the condition that has always been a mystery, even to me, since I've been working here. No two people with Usher are the same; we're an individual bunch. Some can hear better, some can see better, some use canes, some don't, some sign, some lip-read, but all of us live our lives looking out from our own unique tunnels.

Most importantly, though, I've seen just what a difference it makes to people to be able to talk to someone who understands, who's been through the same as them, who knows ways that will make life easier and who can assure them that it *does* get easier. There was no service like this set-up when I was diagnosed, nothing specific to Usher.

And helping other people has perhaps empowered me to make more changes in my own life. Now I'm fully able to embrace this new Jo, and since the break-up of my last relationship, I've decided to move back home to Gateshead. So, at the end of my day in the capital, instead of boarding the train back from London to my office in Wakefield, I'm now sitting here as it whizzes past fields and meadows racing back towards the Tyne, to home.

My eyes catch glimpses of the orange bricks and grey slate

roofs of the mining towns we pass on the way. Like blurry mile-stones they guide the way home for me, those familiar stations that tell me I'm nearing Gateshead.

And then here she is: her arms stretched wide as if welcoming me back home with a huge hug. The Angel of the North stands tall guarding the North-East, signalling safety and all the comforts of home. Mam and I have often taken a walk out to see her from the Chowdene estate where I was brought up. She is like an old friend to me and so many others who have left the North-East: lorry drivers tired from hours up and down the A1, students who've left mams to find their way in the world at university, lovers longing to be reunited with their Tyneside girls. And me, a Geordie at heart, black and white running through my veins and happy memories of a wonderful childhood back home in Gateshead. If I close my eyes, I can still smell the freshly cut grass on summer days in Mam's garden as a child, still picture Granddad's hat and gloves on the dining table as mince and pota-toes steam up the windows of our kitchen, and still see me, Julie and Alana darting in and out of the house as we run up and down the street with our friends, often with a screwball dripping in monkey's blood.

It's not the bullying I remember, or the cruel names, the catty girls, the people who would nip my ankles with supermarket trol-leys because I couldn't hear them asking me to get out of their way. It's home and happiness.

Where else in the world would I choose to live apart from back home in Gateshead?

I feel a dragging sensation as the train starts to press gently on its brakes and we shunt slowly across the Tyne Bridge. I look up out of the window at the beautiful steelwork: another sign of home. These days I can't see as much of her as I once did, just a bit of the arch here and there, not the whole way she bends her protective arm, keeping watch over the two sides of the Tyne like a mother guarding her two precious boys. As we cross the bridge, I marvel at the thick bolts holding fast to the joints, each one solid, strong, identical, there's magic and beauty in that engineering – or perhaps only a Geordie can fully appreciate this beacon of our city.

I've bought a semi-detached house not far from Mam and Dad, but I'm staying with them while the builders bring it up to date.

It's so nice being back in my old bedroom again; there's something safe and comforting about going to sleep and waking up in the same room that made me feel so secure as a child. I take my hearing aids out at night and leave them on the same chest of drawers that I did as a girl.

And there's nothing like the familiarity of the streets that I skipped along when I was little – so much so that I'll leave Matt at home with Dad or won't even get my cane out of my handbag to walk to the bus stop. I know every twist and turn of those pavements, every bump in the concrete, every tree root that crosses my path, so I don't need my white cane to tell me what's beneath my feet back here.

There was a part of me, though, that feared returning home wearing this new label, the blind one. So many people on the Chowdene estate had always known me as the Deaf Girl, but now I would be walking along with a white stick or a guide dog as well as my hearing aids – a deafblind girl.

I worried about those first moments bumping into someone I'd been to school with, with whom I hadn't caught up over the years that had only afforded me snatched weekends home, here and there. I could still remember my shock at seeing my reflection in the coffee shop window. I knew how I would look to their unknowing eyes.

But something else incredible has happened in the last few weeks, which has in fact helped with all that. Because to some extent I've become a bit of a local star.

Just a week ago, I received an email from one of my Sense colleagues saying I'd been nominated for one of the *Daily Mirror*'s Pride of Britain awards. My work as a mentor coordinator, plus some of the fundraising I'd done trekking with Matt, had meant that I'd got down to the last four people out of 20,000 nominated for their Local Hero award.

My cheeks flushed as I read the email, but a little pride swelled in my stomach. I didn't feel like a hero, though. I was just doing what came naturally to me; I'd only ever wanted to help people. It was Matt who'd given me the confidence to get out walking again; together we'd trodden miles and miles of the Peak District, all with the aim of raising thousands of pounds and the profile of Sense.

And we'd achieved that – but the other thing I'd achieved, without even realising it, was bringing my own story to the attention of others. Sense had nominated me for this award – they felt my bravery at dealing with Usher, and the work I'd done helping others with the condition, was worthy of recognition.

'But there are so many other people with Usher who have achieved incredible things too,' I told Mam.

She smiled at me. 'Enjoy your moment, Joanne,' she said.

I think she and everyone else could see how far I'd come, and they wanted me to realise it too. But for me, it had been a difference between simply surviving and finally living. Helping people gave me as much satisfaction as it did them, probably more because I saw them start to sparkle and shine from my own little tunnel. And that was the best view of all.

Today, the local news reporters have come to film me meeting with some of the Usher mentors that I have recruited.

As the cameras roll in our meetings, or as I walk along with Matt for their piece, it finally strikes me just how far I've come too.

And when local people spot me on the news the next day, it means I don't have to see the shock on their faces when they see me out with my white stick. The TV interviews do the job of letting everyone know that the Deaf Girl is now blind.

There is still the odd neighbour whose eyes glisten with tears when they see me again, though. 'It's not fair,' they'll say to me, their lips quivering as I tip my head to one side with a sympathetic smile. The smile is for them, not me – because I am fine.

A few weeks later, I'm told that I haven't won the Pride of Britain award, another worthy winner has been picked, but it isn't the winning that matters to me. The fact that I have embraced the new me, and that everyone has embraced me right back, is reward enough.

There is nothing more thrilling than watching a child open their presents on Christmas Day – tearing off the paper that's been so lovingly and carefully wrapped around the gift, discarding the paper printed Santas and Rudolphs on the floor in exchange for the lure of the present that's inside. I might not be able to hear the squeals of joy, but the look on my niece Casey's face says everything. She is Julie's daughter. Before, because I was living away in Sheffield, I didn't get to see her as much as I'd have liked. But all that's changed now I'm home.

Casey is four now and Christmas means so much to her. And, for the first time in years, to me too – because this year it is loaded with more promise than ever before. I am now just weeks away from an operation that may allow me to hear sound.

I have been having regular appointments with Mr Coulson over the last twelve months. He has seen me through my reintroduction to the working world, my move back to Gateshead, and now he offers me something that may be entirely life changing. When I think of it like that the excitement threatens to bubble up inside me and come flooding out in goosebumps that cover my whole body, and it often does.

But bubbling just underneath the skin is another sensation: the fear of anything going wrong.

Not that I share those worries with anyone; I bury them deep inside. Instead, on the surface, I'm filled with unadulterated joy at the thought of joining this exclusive hearing club that I've been refused entry from for my entire life.

This Christmas holds the same magic as so many before it. The familiar smells wrap around my nose wherever I go, from roasted chestnuts in the winter market in town to the sticks of cinnamon wrapped with red ribbons that decorate the tree.

And being back at Mam's for this time of year, the whole family gathered together, makes it extra-special.

'It's Elsa from *Frozen*!' I lip-read from Casey as she opens the doll that Julie has helped me pick out for her this year.

Her dark eyes are huge and bright as she comes over to thank me, rather than shouting her thank you across the room like she has done with everyone else. Just like the rest of my family before her, Casey has got used to my disabilities. She's grown up knowing that if she says something funny, I won't get it until someone tells me afterwards. When everyone else laughs, I won't know what's happened until someone repeats it – and Casey will be there every time, waiting to laugh again. Like any toddler she enjoys repeating the same story over and over, and her laugh is genuine each time, even if the adults have tired by then. When she giggles, her whole face lights up, her smiles revealing the little gap in her two front teeth that reminds me so much of Julie.

It was hard to communicate with her when she first started speaking. Most parents, even, struggle to decipher what their child is trying to tell them at that stage, but for me it was nearly impossible.

These days, though, now she's four years old, we can have a chat I'll often feel her tiny little hand on my knee, letting me know she needs the full focus of my tunnel to tell me something mightily important about Peppa Pig or one of the characters from *Frozen*.

But there have been some benefits to being a deaf auntie: when Casey was a baby her crying certainly never bothered me!

But here we all are, Christmas morning, the lights dancing on the tree in Mam and Dad's living room, the scene of so many yuletides gone by and happy memories. Julie has put a Christmas CD on, and as we open our presents, Mam, Julie and Alana sing away to songs from the past, swapping memories of when Paul McCartney or Slade was on *Top of the Pops*. Of course I remember watching the performances over and over when I was a girl, Julie pausing the video player to write down or mouth the lyrics to me, but never actually hearing the songs that have become the soundtrack to so many lives.

I feel Julie tap my knee. 'Ee, you'll be able to hear that song next Christmas,' Julie mouths to me, and there are those bubbles and goosebumps again.

As we all sit around, everyone starts talking about the songs that bring back the most memories. Mam starts talking about Elvis's 'Suspicious Minds', closing her eyes as she pictures Dad back in the Majestic in his teddy-boy suit and with his bunch-of-grapes hairdo. Dad is telling me that Journey's 'Don't Stop Believin'' is the track for him, Alana mentions 'Live Forever' by Oasis. It feels like they're all members of this secret club, and I can't imagine what it's like, how just the memory of a song ringing out from the speakers can bring so much happiness to their faces and pictures of years gone by racing to the forefront of their minds. Because, of course, music has never touched me like that. I might have felt the beat, but I've never heard a single note.

'You've got all this to come, pet,' Dad says from his armchair, and it's true, I have. Not long now.

There were some things that I'd pieced together about music. For example, I knew there were different genres like classical or rock music, but only because I had visual clues: a conductor guiding an orchestra, the way a violinist worked her bow. All these were clues that classical music was calm and gentle, as opposed to rock music, where I'd see a singer rocking on the stage, going crazy with his guitar, where the crowds would be on their feet, arms in the air, jumping up and down to the sound.

But of course, I had no idea what that sound was, or what it meant to so many people. Without ever having tasted the notes, I had no idea that they had the power to transport people back to a place or time, to make you feel the same emotions as you had when you were falling in love, or heartbroken. This was what people had told me about music, but I'd never experienced it myself.

And as I sit here now on Christmas morning, I realise there is a whole world of sound to experience. I watch in silence as Casey rips open more presents. Is there a sound to go with that? I might pick up a deep belly laugh from Dad if Casey does something funny, but I've never heard her own little giggle. Or – I glance across the room – Mam's voice.

So much awaits me. And yet . . . I have to realise that the operation could also plunge me into a world of permanent silence: no white noise, no nothing. Because if the operation in just a few short weeks doesn't work, I won't be going back to my hearing aids.

Instead, there really will be silence.

One after another, the bright lights whizz past my eyes. I'm lying on a hospital bed and the porter is wheeling me into theatre. My hearing aids have gone already, so there is nothing but silence as my companion. I can only see the ceiling, the odd flash of strip lighting as I'm wheeled through the hospital corridors, and my stomach is turning over and over. It may be to do with the fact that I've been too nervous to eat for the last twenty-four hours, but then food has been the last thing on my mind, because today is the day for my operation, apparently the start of my new life . . . and yet I could snatch my hearing aids out of the cardboard tray I had to put them in moments ago and run away from this hospital right now.

Mam has come with me to the Queen Elizabeth Hospital in Birmingham, the same one where I've been meeting Mr Coulson and his team for the last twelve months.

Mam chattered away to me on the train last night; she knew that my nerves were getting the better of me so she tried to keep the conversation light. I watched her mouth moving as we sat opposite one another, but what was spilling from her lips was lost on me as my mind took a journey of its own, asking the same questions it has done for almost a year now. Am I doing the right thing? Am I really not all right just the way I am?

When we arrived at the hospital accommodation, Mam busied herself chatting to the other patients who are having operations today. She was her usual cheery, positive self, wishing them well, telling them it would be fine. I'm sure she was convincing herself about my operation as much as reassuring them about theirs.

And then the morning came and we went onto the ward to prepare for surgery. A nurse gave me a gown to slip into, and asked for my hearing aids. I took them out, my security blanket, feeling a strange pull towards these things that had in some ways been the bane of my life, and in others had been there for me for nearly thirty years.

Plunged into silence, I could only watch as Mam chattered away to Mr Coulson, occasionally one or both of them throwing me a comforting smile to make sure I felt included in the conversation, but of course I wasn't. Without the back-up of my hearing aids, the distant mumble that they afforded me, it was impossible to keep up with them. My eyes darted from Mam to Mr Coulson, but it was no use.

My empty stomach started to churn over and over, because I knew this was how life might be after the operation. I faced one month of silence like this before the switch-on, and of course there were no guarantees that it was going to work. There was a slim chance that this world was the one I might spend the rest of my life in, my eyes working tirelessly to keep up with those who could chat so easily around me.

I thought of my hearing aids in that cardboard tray. My eyes quickly scanned the room for them, but my tunnel denied me even a glimpse. Which was probably for the best – because if I could have spotted them, the temptation to plug myself back into my white noise and escape the hospital ward might have proved too much.

So, instead, here I am, gliding through the corridors on this hospital bed. I see a doorframe above me and guess that we're now in the room where they'll give me the anaesthetic. The porter's face appears in my tunnel. 'I'll leave you here now,' he says.

I smile but my heart is racing. The next face I see is Mam's.

'I'll be here when you wake up,' she says. She smiles at me. I want to cry then, the fear of the unknown bubbling up inside and threatening to come spilling out, but I swallow down the hot tears, and instead smile and nod at Mam. 'You'll be OK,' she tries, and then she's gone, out of my tunnel.

I feel alone now, staring up at the ceiling. Without any background noise, I can't hear the hum of people around me. Is anybody there?

But the next face I see is Mr Coulson's, his smiling eyes looking down my tunnel reassuringly. Dressed in his blue scrubs, he looks different to how I've seen him before, but I feel comforted to see a familiar face.

I think back to all the conversations we've had in his office, how many times I've left with the hope that he can turn me from a deaf girl into a hearing one. And now we're here, ready for that moment. I'm about to be given a general anaesthetic, one that could change my life. Will I wake up with working ears? Could it really work? Excitement and fear mingle in my tummy, my heart pumps a little bit harder with the thought, and nerves.

But there's no time for second thoughts now. It is time. Mr Coulson's face disappears and is replaced by another, that of the anaesthetist.

'We're ready for theatre now,' I lip-read. 'I'd like you to count to ten for me.'

I take a breath. This is it.

'One . . . two . . . three . . .'

But the blackness descends before I make it any further.

Chapter Fifteen

My eyelids feel as if someone has attached lead weights to them, but slowly, with great effort, I blink them open. As I do, a crack in the ceiling comes into focus, then a piece of strip lighting, and then, a few moments later, a face – my Auntie Edna. Her face is so warm and welcoming, her smile so broad and reassuring. Edna is Mam's cousin and she's been keeping her company during my seven-hour operation. Edna has been a constant in my life, and it's such a relief to see her here, even though I'm too weary to say hello.

Seconds later, Mam's face appears in my tunnel behind her. Both of them look so happy to see me.

I have enough strength to turn my head towards the window. I see that it's dark. It was early morning when I went into theatre.

My head feels heavy, my body a dead weight, darkness descends as I close my eyes again and fall back to sleep . . .

* * *

My eyes open again, a bit easier this time. Who knows how long I've been sleeping for, but here are those two smiles again in my tunnel: Mam and Edna. I indicate to them to help me sit up. Both of them must jump up to help because slowly I feel myself being lifted under my arms, propped up a bit higher on two firm NHS pillows.

Mam's face appears in my eyeline. 'How do you feel, Joanne?' she asks.

'Did they do the operation? Is it over?' I croak. And Mam and Edna laugh.

Of course they did it. I only have to reach up to my head to touch the bandages that pinch the skin around my forehead. I don't feel in any pain thanks to the anaesthetic that's still swimming around my system, just the pull of the bandages wrapped tightly round my head.

But more than anything, I'm starving. My stomach is empty as nerves stopped me facing any food yesterday. I ask Mam to find me something to eat and she offers me a tuna sandwich. I wolf it down like I haven't eaten for a year, followed by chocolate and grapes. Finally, I lie back against my pillow, sated, and fall back off to sleep . . .

I leave hospital two days later, but before I do, Mr Coulson comes to visit. He tells me that the operation went better than he could ever have hoped for. My heart swells with excitement. I'm one step closer to my dream.

Now, I'm back home in Mam's front room while she and Dad wait on me hand and foot. It reminds me of the days I spent tucked up under the duvet as a child, except back then I would have had my phonic ear for company. I would have heard a gentle hum to tell me if the television was on or a mumble of sounds if Mam was calling to Julie upstairs. Now, without my hearing aids, there is nothing except total and utter silence to keep me company and, as the days have worn on, I've found it a depressing companion.

It's strange that this silence is one that has accompanied me my whole life, and yet I don't feel safe as it walks beside me. Perhaps that's because it has now been joined by my blindness, but without white noise from my ears, my eyes feel more useless than ever. Often a friend will come to visit, and I'll have no idea anyone is in the room until they appear, directly in front of my tunnel. This morning I came downstairs and had no idea that Dad was watching the horse racing until I caught a glimpse of the TV, flickering away in the corner. It's surprising how much those low hums, the tiny bit of background noise that I've got used to, has wrapped me up in a security blanket over the years. Suddenly, without it, I feel lost.

'Why don't we have a little walk outside?' Mam suggests.

We decide to go to see the Angel. It's the beginning of March and we wrap up warm to protect us from the biting cold of a North-East winter. I still have bandages that cover my head; I look a bit like a Teletubby without my woolly hat on, just two extra-thick foam bandages on each side of my head where the implants went in. My head was shaved for the operation too; a flap of skin lifted each side behind my ears to reveal my skull, which was then drilled into to allow them to thread the implant into my cochlea. When I'd first woken up in hospital, I hadn't

205

been in any pain, but as the days go by and the stitches do their job of pulling my scalp back together, the soreness stings at my skin.

It's good that I can stay with Mam and Dad as there's not much I can do for myself, not even make a cup of tea. I've never heard a kettle boil and yet somehow my hearing aids used to deliver me a sign that signalled the kettle had boiled so I didn't burn myself. Without them, life is a mystery. I feel lost and at times scared.

Friends who come to see me talk excitedly about when the implants are turned on, but that seems a long way off yet as I wait in my month of silence. And of course, the bit that scares me the most is the thought of staying like this forever, that this deathly quiet might be a lifelong friend now.

Not that I share those fears with anyone else; everybody is too excited about the new world that awaits me to pour scorn on it. Instead, I busy myself planning how to decorate my new place. It's just weeks until I'll move in, so I plan what colour paint I'll have on the walls, how I'll design my kitchen . . . and all this is just to keep my mind off the real question: will my ears really work for the first time when it comes to the switch-on?

As Mam and I sit beside one another in the hospital waiting room, I think to myself how times have changed. We're all sitting in rows as if facing the front of the class, but the 'teacher' we all have our eyes on is in fact a large widescreen TV, on which is posted each of our names and the waiting time before we'll be seen.

Joanne Milne: ten minutes.

I shuffle awkwardly in my seat, and see Mam do the same,

though neither of us says anything; perhaps we're both too nervous.

Nine minutes.

Just like when I was a child, there is a play area in one corner of the room, except there's more than just an old abacus there now, there are plastic toys with lights that dance and flash. I watch one little boy playing with one such toy, mesmerised. His ears are clearly unable to enjoy the noisy toys that other toddlers are drawn to, but here he has something that stimulates another sense. I smile as I see his mother show him how to make it work, how to change the colours, or make them flash.

Eight minutes.

The screen above us has the names of three other people, all of them with some kind of deafness, and all able to relax in the waiting room because, thanks to the screen, they now know when to look out for someone calling them. I think about how hospitals have changed over the years, how they now make life easier for deaf people, how people are more disability-aware. I think of the hospitals I've attended to check my sight, how alien the yellow signs with thick black writing were to me a few years ago – and how I've now come to rely on them.

Seven minutes.

I cross and uncross my legs. I see Mam wipe her clammy palms on her coat, then fish around in her handbag for a tissue.

Six minutes.

Today is the switch-on day. A day I've been waiting for my entire life, though it never felt like that before now. I had been happy to be a deaf girl – until I realised that there could be more out there for

me. But once I'd started looking into cochlea implants, once I realised there might be a way to turn myself from a deaf girl into a
hearing one, this day couldn't have come soon enough.

Five minutes.

And then there's that nagging fear too, the one that makes my
heart race just a bit quicker, which makes my own palms clammy
and wet. What if the operation hasn't worked?

Four minutes.

If I said that to Mam now, she'd tell me I was being silly, that of
course it has worked. She would offer me reassuring words, the
positivity oozing from her just like it always has.

But as I look down, and see her feet shuffling nervously on the
floor, I know she's thinking the exact same thing as me. We don't
need words; we never have.

Three minutes.

I look up at the screen, and swallow hard.

Two minutes.

I see a door open. Another patient leaves the doctor's room
smiling; she's clutching some paperwork.

One minute.

I'm looking down at the floor when I see a pair of black shoes
appear beside me. I look up, see a friendly face appear in my
tunnel, and feel the vibrations of Mam shuffling to get up next to
me. My heart is racing now as I gather up my handbag and the
coat I've slung over the back of my chair.

'Would you like to follow me, Joanne?' the nurse says. And in
we go.

* * *

In the times that I've been over and over this moment in my mind, it has all happened much more quickly. In my dreams there is one button to press to switch on my implants; in reality this is a three-hour appointment. So as I take a seat opposite the audiologist, Louise, my nerves settle and my heart starts to thump less hard in my chest. She speaks directly into my tunnel to make sure I can understand everything that she's saying. Before she officially switches on my implants, she needs to align each one of the forty-four electrodes with the computer. It's a long, drawn-out process as she attaches wires from my new hearing aids to her computer, and when she puts them behind my ears for the first time they feel cold and hard, a little like how they first felt when I had them as a child.

It takes more than an hour for her to activate the implant and for it to start speaking to the computer. She does each one of the twenty-two in my left ear in turn, asking me to press a button when I hear any kind of sound, and then press it again when it is comfortably loud. The sounds are just low hums, or beeps, nothing different from the other hearing tests I've had over the years. As she goes through the process, checking and double-checking, ticking off from a list, scrawling figures down and adjusting pitch and volume, I think back to the days of putting marbles into a glass jar. There were no fancy computers then, just bulky grey equipment.

I remember the different consultants I've had over the years. Mr Mathias with his big furry eyebrows that fascinated me as a child, how he'd gently get down into my eyeline, speaking straight into my face so I could concentrate as best I could, and yet my eyes would always wander back to those caterpillar eyebrows. I try not to giggle at the memory.

Once every electrode in my left ear has been activated – one at a time, never altogether – Louise repeats the process in my right ear. Mam sits patiently, fascinated instead of bored by the whole process. Again, I press a button every time I hear a sound, and then again when it's comfortably loud.

Then, after it seems that hours have gone by, the same laborious process repeated over and over, Louise puts down her pen and smiles at me.

'Are you ready for me to switch the implants on now?' she asks.

And there it is again: my heart instantly leaps to my throat. This is it . . .

Every hair is standing up on my body, a feeling like electricity is pulsing through me. There's a tingling inside me, a ringing in my ears, my arms, my legs, like no sensation I've ever felt before. It goes all through my body, this tingle, all the way from my head to my toes, and then is swallowed up into the floor.

Every letter and syllable bounces off the walls, the ceiling, the doors, ringing out around the room, in my ears, and rattling round my brain.

The audiologist stopped speaking seconds ago, and yet the sound lingers in the room, long since her lips have stopped moving.

'*Caaaaaan . . . yoooooooooou . . . heeeeeeeeear . . . meeeeeeeeee?*'

The first words I ever heard.

My brain distinguishes every little part of them, trying desperately to keep up, to take them in and then spit out every single new sound that has pirouetted out of the nurse's mouth and hit my ears, exploding like a firework. It darts about and dances inside my head, every single nerve coming alive for the first time with this new sensation: sound.

Is this what I've waited nearly forty years for? Is this what sound is like?

And then I realise: I'm hearing for the first time. This isn't a white noise, a gentle hum, this isn't the faint whisper of a huge belly laugh, or a distant beat as my head is pushed up against a speaker on the highest volume. This is me, Jo, sitting in a room, hearing for the first time. This is what it feels like not to be deaf. This is hearing.

'I'll go through the days of the week,' the audiologist tells me slowly. And as she speaks again, my brain tries desperately to process the words. 'Kkkkk . . .' echoes in the room long after she's finished her sentence. It seems to jump twice my height, then back down again into my ears. Sound moves, it's all around, it's not just something inside my head, it's something I feel throughout my whole body.

My brain is alive as it tries to keep up, processing something it's never had to before. Like jumping into an ice-cold bath on a sunny day, it goes from silence to sound in seconds and it all feels too much.

The audiologist sounds how I've imagined a robot might sound. Her voice is high, squeaky and electronic. Is this how people sound?

She starts to speak again as I nod to indicate I'm ready: 'Monday . . . Tuesday . . . Wednesday . . .'

I'm trying to take in the words but it's too much. The excitement, the emotion come fizzing out of my body like a can of soda, my hands are shaking as the tears pour down my face, over and over, out they come, spilling into my lap as I try desperately to take it all in.

This is what it's like to hear. I am hearing. This is sound.

She carries on: 'Thursday . . . Friday . . . Saturday . . . Sunday . . .'

Words I've known my entire life, but ones I'm hearing now for the first time. Something so ordinary, and yet they are the most beautiful things I've ever heard.

Mam is standing to my right, filming this moment. I go to speak and I have this strange sensation from within. A voice in my head. My own voice.

'It sounds very high,' I say to the audiologist.

'It will sound high-pitched at first,' she says slowly. 'Your brain will readjust it for you. It won't always sound that way.'

I put my head into my lap and sob.

'Sorry,' I cry, putting my head up momentarily.

'It's a big, big, life-changing day,' Louise tells me, and I sob again, because the full impact of it is only just starting to dawn on me. I can hear.

'Can you hear your own voice?' she asks me. I manage to nod. 'Good!' she says.

Like lightning, the 'oo's dance around the room, whipping around my head and twinkling in the air above me, leaving glittery trails as they go. The 'd' shunts behind them, leaving an echo in its path. Firm, strong, hard.

'It sounds very, very strange,' I tell Louise, and the tears come again.

'It will do,' she says. 'You've done so well, Joanne. It's such a huge thing you've just achieved, you should feel really proud of yourself – it's fantastic.'

And I'm drowning in more tears.

'Right, smile,' Mam says, as she stands with the video camera. Mam. Mam's voice. She has been my mouthpiece, my ears, my eyes, my entire life, and I've never even heard how she sounds until now. My brain desperately tries to compute the difference between her and Louise and instantly spots it: Mam's Geordie accent. So that's how we sound.

'Well done,' Louise says. 'It really is a wow moment.'

'It's amazing,' I manage, before the sound of my own voice sets me off again.

Louise must sense this because she asks: 'Can you hear yourself speaking?'

'It's more you,' I tell her. 'It sounds very, very high-pitched.'

'It does at first,' she says. 'But it won't stay like that.'

And then she starts telling me the months of the year, asking me to tell her how the volume is in each ear, and just like the days of the week these ordinary little words seem like the most beautiful things I've ever heard. By the time she gets to November, my face is in my lap, I'm sobbing and sobbing and I feel her hand on my shoulder.

The operation has worked. I can hear. If you could bottle joy at its happiest, that's how I'm feeling right now. I'd never imagined for a moment I could feel like this. In all those years in my silent world, words never sounded like this. They were anonymous, lost on me, strangers that I could only hope to befriend. And yet here I was, hearing.

I put my head down and sob all over again.

I leave Louise's room a hearing woman. As I step out into the waiting room, my tear-stained face must be an instant giveaway that my life has changed in the last two hours. As the door shuts behind us, I hear the click of the wooden frame against the door. As we walk back to our seats I hear the tap of footsteps on the floor. Everything is wondrous to me, the tiny little signs that everyone takes for granted now colour in my world, bringing it to life like I've never experienced before.

It's hard to distinguish what some of the different noises are at first. If I look up and catch a man getting up from his seat, my brain quickly realises that his chair makes a scraping sound as it rubs against the floor. If I look over into the children's corner, I understand that that clattering sound is a child throwing toys back into a box.

Mam watches me, fascinated, and every so often the pair of us giggle.

'What's that noise?' I'll ask her.

'It's a phone ringing behind the desk,' she'll say, and as I look up, my tunnel reveals the receptionist picking up the receiver.

'What's that noise?' I ask again, as a 'clink clink' sound passes by.

'It's a trolley,' Mam says. 'They're delivering sandwiches for lunch.'

Over and over, on and on we go, neither of us able to wipe the broad smiles off our faces.

It's impossible for me to be able to zone in on one noise, so I'm bombarded with everything at the same volume; the receptionist on the phone sounds as loud as Mam sitting next to me. The little toddler having a tantrum in the corner mingles with the announcements over the hospital's loudspeaker asking for porters.

In time, my brain will learn to zone in on one thing, but for now I stare about me, fascinated by the world I've stepped into – a hearing one.

Our work for today isn't over yet, though, and a few minutes later we're called in to see a speech therapist. There, she gives me a chart to look at while she reads words from a separate piece of paper. Each time I've heard the word she says, I'm to point to it on the chart.

She starts: 'Response. Responsible. Responsibility.'

My finger darts from one word to the next as I look down at the chart. I go through rows and rows, over and over, and it's only when I've put the chart down that I realise: I wasn't lip-reading. I wasn't even looking at her.

'You can hear,' she declares, and I hear Mam gasp.

Those words that she's been longing to hear since the hospital appointments she first brought me to as a toddler. Mam bursts into tears and I get up from my seat to give her a hug. I can hear.

We leave the hospital an hour later and head off to get some lunch.

As we step out into the March day, the wind whips around the ground, picking up leaves and swirling them round and round. It pinches at my face, the cold air brushing against my skin. And I realise then that the wind makes a noise, a rushing whoosh of a noise.

'That's the wind, isn't it?' I say to Mam, my eyes alive with delight.

'Yes,' she says. How often must she have stepped out on a windy day with me and heard the same sound, yet here I am at thirty-nine, hearing it for the very first time.

We go to a restaurant and order pasta. It's there, for the first time, that I realise just how noisy the world is. As Mam and I sit and chat – I still can't get used to that – I hear the clattering of the kitchen, knives and forks tapping on plates, the hum of conversations across the room, the fact our glasses clink when we make a toast to my new life. My brain mentally notes down a generic 'restaurant' noise. And then I notice something else: the sound of my own cutlery scraping against my plate.

'I'm a very noisy eater,' I laugh to Mam. She tells me I always have been, and yet I wasn't to know that knives and forks make scraping sounds when they hit china plates. People just adapted around me.

Everything is wondrous to me: the fact that I answer the waitress when she asks if I want Parmesan, even though I'm looking down; the way my glass makes a noise when I put it down on the table too heavily; the ice that clanks around between the lemon slice in my drink. I thought drinks were silent. I thought glasses didn't make a noise. I thought you could only communicate with someone when you were looking at them.

These are all secrets that the hearing world is now letting me in on, and I eat them up along with my pasta. And when my tummy is full, my appetite for sound is far from sated: I could eat and eat all day long.

By the time we get back to our room, though, my brain is exhausted from the effort of hearing. As Mam hangs her coat up in the wardrobe, I ask her for the first time in my life to be quiet.

'Oooh, sorry!' she says. And we both collapse into fits of giggles.

I take my processors off for a rest, and I'm instantly plunged into silence again. I pick them up and pop them back on. And there is sound: the squeak of the mattress as Mam sits on her bed, the whooshing of the toilet after she's flushed it.

Mam and I giggle all night as my eyes light up at other sounds I haven't heard before.

And then finally, when I'm far too tired for anything else, I take out my hearing aids, just like I always have done, and put them on my bedside table so I can sleep.

But as I close my eyes, there is one thing I can still hear: the speech therapist today when she said to me, 'You can hear.'

Chapter Sixteen

Click . . . click . . . click . . . click . . . click . . .

I'm smiling.

Click . . . click . . . click . . .

I start to giggle.

I'm standing in the hallway back at home. On alternate seconds, it's plunged into darkness as the bulb hanging down from the ceiling lights up . . . and goes black . . . lights up . . . and goes black.

On and off the light goes, but it's not the fact that I'm standing here, just inside the front door, in turns in darkness and light that amuses me – but the sound it makes. Who knew light switches had a sound?

Sound, I still can't get used to that word.

Click . . . click . . . click . . .

On and on I go, like a toddler, amused and fascinated in equal measure by such simple things. The last 24 hours of being able to hear really has been like discovering the world again from scratch.

Back in Birmingham, Mam and I had gone back to the hospital the next day to adjust the volume on my implants and make sure everything was still working OK. I'll have several appointments like this over the next few months as the volume on my world is slowly turned up, each time allowing the brain to keep up.

The truth is, though, that my implants are working better than OK: they are truly wonderful. Mr Coulson has given me a gift that no one will ever be able to comprehend. My world has suddenly been switched on right in front of me. A sense I thought I'd never have the pleasure of experiencing, that I hadn't even realised just how much I'd missed, had in an instant coloured and changed and literally lit up my world.

And that's what it's like for me now, standing here in my hallway. This might just be a simple light switch, but it represents my world going from darkness to light. Who knew a light switch had a sound? I laugh to myself again.

But it's not just that. As I walk around my house, a place I know so well, I'm amazed that this place that I once considered such a sanctuary is actually alive with noise.

I'd woken up this morning in our hotel in Birmingham with a tingly feeling in my belly. My eyes soon found the source of such excitement – my two magnetic coils perched on the bedside table. My hands reached out for them before I'd even wiped the sleep from my eyes, and popped them behind my ears, the magnet in the implant embedded in my skull automatically connecting to the one disguised in my hair.

And there it was: sound.

I lay there in bed for a long time before Mam woke up, smiling to myself as I listened to the first morning ever in my life, to the sound of the world waking up. Everything from the voices of people staying in the neighbouring hotel rooms to the scratchy sound my duvet made when I rolled over was absolutely fascinating to me. I coughed, and had to stifle a giggle. My cough, *my* noise.

I could hear Mam sleeping, her soft breath making tiny whistling sounds, and when she started to wake up, I could hear her legs shuffling under her own duvet, and then one beautiful sound: 'Morning.'

Mam.

I couldn't stop smiling for a second as I went about my morning routine, doing things on automatic that I've done every day of my life and yet now they took on a whole new dimension. The *whoosh* of water bursting from the shower as I turned it on before I stepped in; the *squirt* as I squeezed cleansing gel into my hand; the *swish* inside my head as I brushed my teeth.

Every single sound I hear delights, amuses and amazes me. I never want this feeling to go away, and I have to keep reminding myself: it won't. This is me now. This is Joanne Milne.

The label that has defined me my entire life has gone in an instant.

Back at the hospital, they were happy with how the implants were working, so that was it. Off Mam and I went, chattering all the way back on the train.

I can't help but notice that I'm still lip-reading, that my eyes can't easily be drawn away from lips that they've spent their entire lives following intently. The audiologist told me this is natural, that it might be a habit that takes years to break, but there's no doubt that I can hear.

Sometimes it surprises me, though, when I realise just how quickly my brain has become accustomed to sound, like when I caught myself fishing in my handbag for my train ticket on the way home, just because – I realised – I must have heard the inspector coming along shouting, 'Tickets please!' And then I giggled again to myself.

Back at Newcastle Station, Mam and I jumped into a taxi.

Clunk, the big black cab door slamming shut, another sound to add to the library my brain is quickly acquiring.

Mam dropped me off first at my place, while the taxi's engine chugged over and over as we said our goodbyes. And as I walked up my drive, noticing that the gate made a little metallic squeak as I pushed it open, there was a part of me that was longing for the silence that lay beyond my front door. For as wonderful as it was spending every second immersed in sound, it was actually very tiring for my poor brain to keep up with after almost forty years of silence.

I wanted to get inside and experience the peace that living alone affords me.

And yet, here I am now . . . *Click, click, click, click* . . . My house is anything but silent. Footsteps on my newly installed lime-washed laminate floor follow me everywhere I walk, leaving an echo that lingers in my minimalist home instead of being soaked up by carpets and curtains.

It takes me ages to work out what the constant buzzing sound in my kitchen is, until I trace it to the fridge. I'd always thought of it as such an inanimate object; who knew it had a heart buzzing away inside? I open up the freezer and hear the *chhuuuuush* that accompanies the icy air that pours from its drawers.

There's the constant *ticktock* of clocks, the *tapping* of the central heating, the voices of children playing outside and cars rumbling past, a dripping tap. The *squeak* of leather as I sit down on my sofa, or the *whoosh* of air as I take off my coat and hang it on a peg.

I go to get myself a drink from the kitchen, remembering to put the glass that I take from the cupboard down gently, so it doesn't clatter on the worktop. I pour myself a glass of sparkling water, and suddenly I hear this fizzing sound all around me.

Fizzzzzzzzz ... I look behind me, on the floor, above me. *Fizzzzzzz* ... And then I look down at my glass, see the bubbles jumping and skipping and dancing on top of the water, and my brain pieces it together. So this is what sparkling water sounds like.

I giggle again to myself, and then giggle again at the sound of my own voice.

It's only once I'm lying in bed that night, when I've switched the implants off, that I'm once again plunged into silence around me – but not inside, because my mind is whirring with different noises that linger long after I've placed the hearing aids next to me on my bedside table.

The moon casts a streak of light on them, and I smile.

Suddenly, I can't wait until morning.

*　　*　　*

My friend Tremayne walks in and puts his keys down on the worktop in my kitchen, just like he has done a million times before. Except this time, I jump because they make a loud, clattering noise as he does it.

Even though I've just let him into the house with our usual greeting, both of us realise in that moment that there's something very unusual about today. The sound of the keys has reminded us that I've never even heard the voice of one of my closest friends before.

Tremayne is part of my very close group of friends; we jokingly call ourselves The Gang. There's quite a few of us, all close friends. It started off with Richard and Zoey, whom I met around the time of working at Hunters Moor; they'd be the ones on the dance floor trying to convince people I was actually deaf even though I was dancing away to the music like anyone else out there, illuminated by the disco lights.

There's lots of us in our gang including Deb and Janvier and Angela, Tremayne's wife.

Most of us have jobs working in nursing or in support care – Tremayne, for example, works with the hard of hearing, designing loop systems that people can use to amplify their hearing aids in banks and post offices.

But while everyone might do different jobs, one quality they all have is an incredible zest for life, and they have always been so inclusive of me as their deaf friend.

They are the ones who have wiped my tears away when relationships have ended, who've had the forethought to buy light-up necklaces and miners' helmets when we've been camping, so I'd still be able to lip-read once darkness fell. They are the ones who rotate themselves around me at a pub table so I'll get a chance to talk to everyone in turn, instead of trying to keep up with a group conversation. They are the ones who invite me to Janvier's gigs and never think that just because I'm deaf I can't join in.

Except, now things have changed, and today Tremayne has organised something very special to celebrate that. Today, I will hear music for the first time.

He has compiled a playlist for me. This will be the first music I will ever hear – and, better still, I will hear it for the first time in front of the nation.

A few weeks ago, Tremayne tweeted in to Lauren Laverne at her 6 Music show and asked if my story could be featured in a slot called Memory Tapes. There's always a story behind why people pick the music they do, and today it will feature someone who has never heard music before – me.

'Are you ready?' Tremayne says, as I fiddle with my hair in front of the mirror.

Sshhhhhh, the can of hairspray says as I spritz it into place. I look at the can and at the mirror. I didn't know hairspray had a noise.

But apparently, we can't be late.

'We're live on air in 30 minutes,' Tremayne says as we get into his Jeep. *Rattle*: the engine starts up and off we go to his house. As we go over the flyover beside the Tyne Bridge, Tremayne is talking to me but I'm not taking it in. *Whoosh*: a car whizzes by ours. *Clinkle clankle*: the sound of the chains at the backs of the lorries. *Clunk clunk*: Tremayne's car's indicator as we pull off the main road and turn into his street.

At his place there are more new sounds to get used to. He makes us drinks as I sit in the living room. The fridge door opening . . . Milk being poured into a cup . . . The rumble of the kettle boiling . . . And finally footsteps as he returns back into the room with two steaming hot cups of tea.

And it's only now, plonking himself down next to me on the sofa, that he notices the tears rolling down my cheeks, because it's right now, in this moment, that I realise I'm not only less deaf anymore, I'm less blind too.

From another room, I'd been able to have a picture in my mind of what he was doing when he was gone. I could see, even though Mr Coulson had only made my ears work. And it feels incredible.

'Come on,' he says, wrapping me in a hug. 'You're going to be OK. I'll talk for you on the radio.'

And, seconds later, we're live on air to the nation.

Imagine hearing something so powerful, a sensation so overwhelming, that every little nerve inside you tingles and comes alive. Each tiny hair stands on end as the sound enters your ears before diving headfirst into your bloodstream and swimming around in your veins, touching every single part of you as it goes. Emotion swells in your heart and deep inside your belly until finally your brain gives way to this flooding of the senses and, before you know it, you're lost, swimming in sound, weightless, floating, moving with it.

This is me now as I sit in Tremayne's North Tyneside living room listening to music for the first time. It is nothing like I had imagined.

I think of all the times as a child I had pushed my head up against the speaker, how the faint beat that sounded hundreds of miles away from my eardrum was, to me, music, or something to move to on a dance floor in Ibiza, a sound I was convinced was something like the one that makes so many people laugh or smile or cry. And yet, it turns out, I knew nothing.

Music is not something that you hear, it's something that you *feel*. And right now, I'm falling in love with it for the first time.

My heart is dipping and darting with its beat, the words are streaming in through my ears and tickling my heart, my whole body wants to move along with the rhythm and my feet want to tap.

This is what music sounds like.

As I'm taken along on this crest of a wave, I have no idea that the nation has come along for the ride with me. That they too have put down their work, their cups of tea, or even the children, to listen along to the first four songs I'll ever hear, and, as they do, try to imagine what it might be like if you'd never heard music before – something that everyone else can just take for granted.

Tremayne has picked one song from every year of my life for my playlist, that's thirty-nine songs in total, and the show has picked four of them to play on air. The first one is Bat For Lashes' 'Laura'.

As the first notes ring out, my skin starts to tingle.

'What's that?' I whisper to Tremayne, longing for him to

identify the instrument that I've probably known all my life but I've never once heard. My eyes dart one way and another, desperate for the visual clues I've spent my whole life relying on, but of course this is radio: there are none.

'Piano,' he replies. And as I start to listen to the gentle song, my heart lifting along with each crescendo, I can't stop the tears.

Tremayne doesn't take his eyes off me. This moment must be almost as wondrous for him as it is for me. And so far, the music he's chosen is more than doing its job.

The next song is Elbow's 'One Day Like This', and as the violins start and the beat kicks in, before anyone has even sung a note, the tears are streaming down my face and my hands are shaking. So this is what I've been missing.

I put my head back and drink in the song, letting it take me along with it on its beautiful journey. As the song reaches its climax, and Tremayne tells me I can hear an orchestra, my skin is covered in goosebumps. It feels in those few seconds as if I've been granted a brand-new life, a new chance, a new beautiful start.

And on it continues. The tinny beat of The Joy Formidable's 'Whirring'. The funky sound of Deee-Lite's 'Groove Is in the Heart'.

Even Lauren Laverne admits live on air that she is in tears listening to my memory tapes, and what I don't know then is this: so is everyone else who is listening. My story is trending on Twitter, Caitlin Moran and even Bat For Lashes herself are tweeting about it. And all the time, I'm sitting in a tiny lounge in the North-East, doing something as simple as listening.

As Tremayne and I sit there in the minutes afterwards, both of our faces red and tear-stained, I manage to squeak a thank you to him for picking out such wonderful songs. And while they might have ended, the memory of them lingers, and I know, like so many people before me, that whenever I hear any of those songs again, they will take me back to sitting right here, in Tremayne's living room, and hearing music for the first time.

And suddenly it all makes sense – why Mam talks about meeting Dad whenever she hears Elvis. Because that's what music does, it transports you to a different time and place. Perhaps it's the closest thing to a time machine we'll ever have – or in our hearts at least.

As my story has caused such a stir, Tremayne uploads the video Mam made of me hearing for the first time onto YouTube, so people who'd been moved by my story on 6 Music could see a little more of my journey.

That afternoon, exhausted from the emotion of it all, my brain overwhelmed with all the beautiful sound, I go home and take my implants out to sit in silence. Peace and quiet greet me like old friends.

I'm lying here in my bed, once again in my silent world. I haven't yet properly opened my eyes, but nevertheless there is a wide smile plastered across my face as the memories of yesterday come flooding back into my newly conscious mind. Music. I had never heard anything so beautiful.

After a few more minutes of silence, my mind revelling in the memories, I check my clock – 8.24 a.m. – and slowly reach for my implants. Only, as I plug them in, as the world comes into focus in my ears, there's a strange sound.

Bang! Bang! Bang! There is shouting, commotion, coming from outside. At the same time, I hear the *buzz buzz* of my phone vibrating. I check it and see I have dozens of missed calls. I go to the window, pull back the thick curtains, and gasp at the scene below. There must be at least ten people on my drive, strangers, reporters, men with cameras, and among them all a familiar face: Mam.

'What's going on?' I wonder aloud, the sound of my own voice startling me still.

I grab my dressing gown and, wrapping it around me, I run downstairs and open the front door as Mam dashes in.

'What's going on?' I ask her.

'It's your video,' she says, breathlessly. 'The whole world has seen it overnight.'

It takes a while to get her in, and for her to explain, but the video that Tremayne had uploaded of me hearing for the first time has gone viral. Nearly two million people have watched it; my story is featuring on news websites all over the world; it's the lead story on the *Mail* Online and on the BBC. The press have been on Mam's doorstep since seven that morning.

'You're famous, Joanne,' Mam jokes. But as I look outside at the reporters who line my drive, I realise she might just be right.

I pick up my phone, finally looking at the messages. People from all over the globe have been trying to contact me: family in Australia, friends in New York, even Ashfiya in Bangladesh – the video has had an impact even there.

I spend that morning doing one interview after another while Mam makes cups of tea for the reporters. Every single news channel wants me on, people want to know more about me, my story;

there is talk of books, of films, even. For me, though, newly woken from sleep, it feels like I am still dreaming. I haven't even got used to the hearing world myself; it's still only thirty-six hours since the implants had been switched on for me. I haven't had time to think how I feel or to describe my favourite sounds, but the world is ready to celebrate with me nonetheless.

Finally, that afternoon, as the last reporter leaves my house, I shut my door and sit down, ready for some peace. But just as I do, I hear the now-familiar squeak of the gate on my driveway.

On automatic, now armed with these 'hearing' clues, I get up and walk over to the front window. As I do, I see two more visitors – but these two fill my heart with joy, and even though I'm exhausted, I feel my energy restored. It's Julie, with little Casey skipping down the drive beside her. The moment I've been waiting for.

I open the door and hear my big sister say hello to me for the first time in my life, and before I've had a chance to contain my feelings, the emotion is spilling out of me while I'm still standing on my doorstep. She wraps me up in a big hug, just like she has so many times before, but this time I hear her say in her Geordie accent in my ear: 'Are you OK?'

She's not interested in the media, only me, as protective as she was when I couldn't hear a thing. Casey skips around the kitchen, oblivious to all that's going on around her. She pushes the breakfast bar stool to one side to get up on the seat; as she does I hear it scrape across the floor. She starts to draw, her crayons rattling in a box, these little sounds all colouring in the world my niece lives in, the everyday things that I haven't been a part of before.

Julie has brought me a sandwich round, so convinced was she that I wouldn't have had time to eat. We sit in the living room and eat them off our knees. And then I hear the scrape of the breakfast bar stool, light footsteps heading towards me, and then Casey is here in front of me, tapping my knee in the way to which she's become accustomed.

'Auntie Joanne,' she says. 'Where are the biscuits?'

Such a simple question, but surely the most beautiful thing I'll ever hear: the voice of my four-year-old niece, all her sweetness and innocence wrapped up in one sentence.

I answer her clearly as the tears prick the backs of my eyes. My heart has never felt so filled up with happiness.

The man standing on my doorstep I have known my entire life, and yet I have never once heard his voice. Dad.

But right at this moment, there aren't any words said at all.

There are none needed.

Dad wraps me up in the biggest hug he's ever given me in his life. He puts his arm around that little deaf girl and says goodbye to her, because here I am, all grown up and hearing. And he doesn't have to say anything, because I can see it in his eyes; he is so, so happy for me.

As he holds me, I feel his heart pump harder, his breathing get that little bit heavier, and I know his prayers have been answered.

'Aye man, I nee yee'd be alreet,' he says finally. 'Ha'way, ya Mam's got sum dinner on.'

And I follow him out to the car. I've been interviewed by so many men over the last couple of days, and yet, hearing my dad's

voice for the first time, never have my Geordie roots felt so embedded in me. He is the head of the family, the man of the house: this
is what a real man sounds like. My dad.

I climb into the car, and as I do, I spot my Alana in the back.
She doesn't make a fuss, she knows I'm still me, but I see her eyes
twinkling with tears, a little more than I've ever seen them before.
She sounds like Dad, Julie and Mam, that same Geordie accent,
and as we speed back to Mam's for mince and dumplings, I forget
about the world's media, because I've never felt more part of my
own family as I do right now.

Chapter Seventeen

Right now, I'm riding on Tyneside Metro. It is something I've done many times before, on automatic, without thinking, accompanied by a white cane or, more recently, Matt. I did it as a child on our family trips to 'the coast', with Julie dressed up to the nines on our way to a night out, and with partners whom I couldn't stop smooching as we passed through each stop. And yet today it feels as if I'm riding the Metro for the very first time. Because today I'm experiencing the *sound* of the Metro for the very first time.

'Doors closing,' the robotic voice announces, as the sliding doors flash into life and close before me. I flinch a little; I'm prepared for the flashing warning lights, the subtle visual signs like people moving their bags or themselves just an inch or so out of the way, but the sound of the voice is new to me.

'The next stop is Jesmond . . . The next stop is South Gosforth . . . The next stop is Longbenton . . .'

On and on it goes, words that I'd spent my whole life being so familiar with, and yet I'd never heard.

'Looong-Bentonnn,' I repeat under my breath. Somehow, simultaneously, I feel a sense of home and that I'm an alien who has landed as a stranger in my own life. It is comforting to hear these words, and yet I feel like I don't quite belong to them anymore, or they to me. That these places aren't mine in the same way I always thought they were. They sound the same and yet different – but then had I ever really been able to imagine what they did sound like? As I'd never heard sound, it was impossible of course to imagine it.

And, whatever I've imagined, it certainly isn't the same as what I'm hearing now, and that's what sets me off again, that's what makes my throat constrict with emotion: this huge fear of the unknown, this feeling of having to start again in a world I thought I knew so well, of stepping out into the daylight blinking like a toddler, unsure, unsteady, so much more unknowing than I had assumed.

By the time I get off, my mouth is dry and I am in tears. Tremayne is waiting for me on the platform; instinctively he wraps me in a giant hug. I think he, more than anyone, has some idea of the noisy world I've been thrust into, how with every second of hearing something new it is both bewildering and exciting and frightening and overwhelming.

There have been moments in the last few days which have made me jump in fright; the sound of my mouth crunching on a crisp I'd just fished from the foil packet in my hand. I hadn't expected eating crisps to be such a sensory experience, to be so loud. The *crunch* rang out in my head, my ears, my mouth, and my skin prickled with the short tiny shock of adrenaline the shock had given me. It sounds silly, doesn't it? A packet of crisps I've perhaps eaten without thinking every day suddenly taking on a whole new meaning for me, becoming a new experience.

But there have been so many firsts for me, not least getting recognised as the 'deaf' woman from the news in the street, and the countless messages on Twitter and Facebook, from friends, from stars. Somebody even wrote to me at home: *To the lady in Newcastle that got to hear after forty years – as seen on TV*, they'd addressed the envelope. And, incredibly, that letter still found its way to me.

All of the people writing to me are saying the same thing: what an inspiration I am, how they cried tears for me watching that video that Mam filmed. I appreciate each and every one of them who has taken the time to write. I am overwhelmed that my story has touched so many people, and not only that, that it has raised such awareness for Usher.

Now people are contacting Sense, asking if I can be their mentor. People who have existed in a deafblind world, locked away, perhaps in a depression like I was for so long are now realising that there is a life out there waiting for them, just like I did.

When I think back to those wasted years I spent under a black cloud of depression, it seems like another me, or at least another lifetime. I can't imagine the Jo that cried in the bath, or was so scared of taking out a white stick. That woman who stood numb with shock outside the hospital, clutching a letter saying she was registered blind, doesn't feel like me now, as I'm off out to meet the rest of my friends. But she is also what brought me to this point; she's also the reason I was brave enough to have the operation.

I only wish I'd had it sooner . . .

That silent regret hangs in the air before Tremayne snaps me out of it by taking my arm and leading me off the Metro platform.

The Gang are throwing me a special party tonight to celebrate the miracle of the last few days.

Tremayne takes me back to his home. There, Angela, Janvier and Debs, the friends I haven't yet had time to see – let alone hear – wrap me in a gigantic group hug. Just like Dad, no one can find the words to express how we all feel. We desperately want just to pick up where we left off, to carry on as if nothing has changed . . . and yet everything has changed in the last few days.

'You sound different,' each of them says to me, though none of them can put their finger on why or how. Perhaps I speak more quietly now my own voice rings out so loud in my head, or maybe hearing how words are pronounced for the first time has already got my brain adjusting my interpretation of them. I am still reeling from the fact I have a Geordie accent, and yet I hadn't heard what that had even sounded like until four days ago.

I sit down on the sofa, and the cat appears by my side, *purring*. A cat's purr; I never knew they made a sound. And yet as it pads around the room, I can see this cat that I've met a thousand times before more clearly than ever, because I can hear when he's coming, the *tap tap* of his claws on the laminate floor, the gentle rattle of his purr as he comes closer.

And even here, with my friends now, I'm amazed at how the individual sounds of their voices assault my senses as my brain desperately tries to decipher each of them.

For the first time in our friendship, I notice how Angela, a fellow Geordie, has a slightly different twang to her accent, presumably because she spent the first seven years of her life between Germany and England . . . information they've told me over the years quickly filling in the blanks, a detective doing its work. I'm amazed to hear that Debs sounds just like my sisters.

Richard, perhaps the one whom I've known the longest, is at work when I first arrive. But suddenly I hear – *I hear* – the

237

doorbell, and then he walks into the room. I've been longing to hear what my closest friend sounds like since the minute the implants were turned on, and now, here he is . . .

We smile at each other from across the room, and I wait, knowing it's coming, the voice of a friend who's been there from the very beginning. Any second . . . Any second . . .

'Hey,' he says finally. 'Come and give me a hug.'

He holds out his arms and I step into them, but as I do my mind is whirring, still drinking in his beautiful soft Scottish accent, the lilt of the words, the way they curl in his mouth and come toppling out in a purr not dissimilar to the cat's.

This is my Richard. I've always known he was from Scotland, but I didn't know he was Scottish. How could I possibly know what that sounded like?

My cheeks are filled with fire and excitement, and happy tears prick my eyes. I may be like an excited toddler, finding my way in a new world, but, wrapped up in my best friend's arms, I don't need to be afraid.

There must be some things that a hearing person takes for granted; perhaps birdsong is one of them. When was the last time they stopped and listened, really listened, to the birds chattering in their garden? I have seen them there my whole life, hopping from branch to branch on the trees in Mam's garden, flying high through the sky. I've seen their little beaks open and shut in chatter that remained a secret to me, until today.

Right now, I'm standing in pitch-black darkness. It's 4.45 a.m. on a cold and crisp April morning. The sun might be about to come up, but right now the coldness bites. My breath leaves a steamy trail in the air; it lingers in front of the tartan scarf I've wrapped myself up in for this morning's adventure. It was far too early when I dressed this morning for my contact lenses, so instead I'm sporting my Buddy Holly specs, and I'm waiting for something very special: the dawn chorus.

Like many people, Chris Watson, a sound recordist with the BBC's *Springwatch*, had been fascinated by my story. And so, he'd invited me here to hear the dawn chorus for the first time, as he filmed both it and me.

This isn't the first TV I've recorded, though. A few days ago, I was sat on ITV's *This Morning* sofa with Holly Willoughby and Phillip Schofield as they asked me to describe the switch-on.

I felt so proud to be able to speak to the nation about Usher; something most people had probably never heard of before. But now, those viewers who had heard my story would be thinking about it; it might be on their minds all day. Perhaps it would make them grateful to be able to hear, to see. I know my story is making so many people ask themselves what it would be like to hear music for the first time, or their partner's voice, or a child's laugh. And all the while, every day, I'm having experiences like this. And so many people want to be there when I have another 'first', and this is why I'm here today, in a park, before dawn breaks.

All is silent as I arrive to meet Chris. We're handed miners' hats so I have some light shining out from the dark, and then we wait for the birds to wake in Saltwell Park. It's a wooded area near my home, one I've jumped and leapt and skipped in so many times before, the same one where I'd take Vance and he'd refuse to get back on the harness, yet on this morning, in the darkness, it has an eerie feeling as the trees cast a moonlight shadow on the ground, and their branches reach up like crooked witches' fingers.

There's a whole crew here as we wait for our feathered friends to wake. And then . . . Chris's face lights up in time with my own at the first little chirp, a *twit twit twitter* which he identifies as a blackbird . . . Now a crow . . . Each with its own unique voice. On and on it goes, getting louder and louder as the sun makes its daily debut on the horizon, bathing the day in light. The sky turns from an inky black to midnight blue, and then slowly brightens as the clouds are streaked with pinks and golden yellows that shimmer all around us.

The dawn in itself is amazing, but it's the birds we're here for and what a performance they put on: calling out good morning to one another like dozens of feathery alarm clocks, Chris pointing out each one, until they harmonise and the beauty in their song, which has rung out every single day of my life and yet eluded me, brings tears to my eyes.

Another one of the firsts that takes my breath away.

It's moments like this, when I think of how this song has been sung every day, that make the regret rise in my throat. This operation, for all the risks that came along with it, has changed my life in an instant. It wouldn't be normal if I didn't wish that I hadn't had it done years ago.

I suddenly feel sad that there's not a special song that takes me back to the moment a partner first said they loved me, or a time in my life when I was most happy. I think of Granddad and wish more than anything that I had been able to hear his voice, for me to have *heard* him say how proud he was of me, rather than just seeing the words leave his lips.

And even in all this excitement and happiness, even in a moment like this, when I'm hearing birdsong for the first time, if that regret creeps up and taps me on the shoulder, I still feel sad for all the moments I've missed that could have been mine much earlier on.

But then, on the other hand, that deaf girl *is* who I was – and she's the reason that I fight for the rights of other disabled people, she's the one who values her sight rather than taking it for granted because she was already without another sense.

If I hadn't known what it was like to be deaf, would I appreciate moments like this now? Would I see them as the precious gift that they are?

And then my throat relaxes, and the tears change their mind about spilling from my tear ducts. No, I was happy the way I was, I was happy being deaf. I just didn't realise how much happier I would be to hear.

I am standing backstage at a Dutch TV show, among the lights and cameras and the wires that zigzag along the floor, as the host desperately googles a song he wants me to hear for the first time.

He's frantically searching through his phone. 'Wait one second!' he says, as his fingers type in the artist's name, and I giggle because I can see just how excited he is to share with me another first. His handsome smile spreads across his whole face at the thought of introducing me to such a huge iconic singer.

In the last few days, my story has gone global. There have been nearly 3 million views of the YouTube clip of me hearing for the first time. I have been in all of the newspapers – and not only in the UK but abroad, too.

That's why I'm here now, having just done an interview on Dutch TV. I flew to Holland this morning after my incredible experience of hearing birdsong, and although I'm exhausted from the travel, and my head is spinning with so many new sounds – the roar of the plane's jet engine, the *bing bong* of the captain's announcement – I stand patiently until Humberto Tan finds the Bob Marley song he so desperately wants me to hear.

It had been a new experience walking through an airport as a 'hearing person'. It wasn't just the new sounds; I also cast my mind back and pictured myself stepping out of the plane at JFK Airport, unfolding my cane for the first time, a publicly deafblind woman for the first time, and a thousand memories came flooding back. Of course I had my cane with me at Amsterdam Schiphol Airport too, but I felt none of the anticipation of shame I had done before because now I had another sense in working order.

And yet, when I heard someone behind me say, 'Excuse me!' I didn't immediately jump out of the way. Perhaps I've been used to people walking around me, used to them seeing the white stick and realising I'm disabled, although these days I'm feeling much more able than I did a few weeks ago. Just being able to hear makes it easier to see. The sounds that hit my ears colour in the blanks for my eyes, giving me a better view of the world around me, even if my tunnel means mine is restricted right down to something smaller than a letterbox these days. If I can hear there are children running around me, I know to be more careful where I step. So perhaps it was because I was concentrating so hard on all these little clues that I forgot to move out of the way when someone called.

'Got it!' Humberto cries, as he finds the song he wants me to hear. We'd got chatting about Bob Marley when we came off air and he spotted the tattoo on my arm. He'd asked me where the words came from and was staggered when I told him I hadn't yet had time to listen to the man who had inspired me to have a permanent indelible reminder of how lucky I am inked on my arm.

Humberto has picked 'One Love', and as it starts to ring out from the tinny speaker on his phone, we start to have a silly playful dance to the beat. So this is reggae. I move with the music, as does my new Dutch friend, and laugh along with him as he watches the delight register on my face.

I realise then, in that moment, that whenever I hear this song in the future it will always take me back to that day – that minute – dancing with Humberto backstage at a Dutch TV show. This is how memories are made, and I am making them.

In the last few days, so many people have recommended songs for me to listen to; there has even been a campaign started by Sense called Song for Jo to encourage people to write in with the song they think should be one of my firsts.

I do feel pressure to catch up with a whole lifetime's worth of music. I know people want to share with me their special songs that take them back to wonderful moments in their lives, and now, finally, I can see what makes that so special to them.

But not only have people been recommending music, they've been writing it for me, too. One man took the time to compose a piece of music called 'As Silence Ends'; another wrote a song called 'Only She Knew'; other strangers have even sent me classical concert tickets. I'm amazed at people's generosity, and it dawns on me just what an impact music has on people that they are so desperate to share it with me.

But as I've started to dip my toe into this beautiful world, there have been moments where it has made me sad, such as the first time I heard 'Danny Boy', the song Granddad used to sing with me as I skipped alongside him on our way to the bus stop. I'd never heard it before and yet it felt familiar, a reminder of Granddad, and the tears welled in my eyes.

I felt sad when I heard 'The Reflex' by Duran Duran, picturing me as the little deaf girl who had painstakingly learnt every single word by lip-syncing off her sister. How proud I had been to be able to sing it, and how it had amused the people that heard me. And yet until I heard it for myself, I had no idea just what I was missing out on; just what I thought I knew when I didn't have a clue.

There was an overwhelming sadness when I heard John Lennon's 'Imagine' too. His lyrics touched me somewhere so deep and I couldn't wait to hear more of his music. And then, when I asked about him, I was told he'd died in 1980. It was almost like grieving for someone for the first time – well, I was. I'd only just got to know him through his music, and yet I was having the news broken to me that there would be no more music from him.

It was the same for a lot of people I heard in those early days: Elvis, Jimi Hendrix, Amy Winehouse, Michael Jackson. Even if I'd seen news coverage of their deaths at the time, my sense of loss that they would never again make music was newly wrought. It made me sad for people who'd gone before I could even get to know them; this is what I'd missed out on, spending all these years in silence. But, equally, I had a chance to make up for it now, which felt exciting and overwhelming in equal measure.

And – I will admit – there were some times during those first few weeks when I just longed for silence. When, despite appreciating every single note that hit my ears, I longed to be alone in my house, to take the implants out from behind my ears and just rest in silence.

It had been a world I'd spent my entire life trying to escape, and yet now it *was* my escape. Silence was suddenly a place where I felt safe again, where I didn't have to keep up, or feel sad, or even feel happy. Where there was no pressure to try and catch up on a lifetime of music. There was just me, at home in my own head, nothing and no one. The silence I'd been so terrified of my entire life suddenly became a great comfort.

Chapter Eighteen

The fly glides through the air as I watch, mesmerised. *Bzzzzzzzz* . . .
On and on it goes. Its tiny transparent wings criss-crossed with
rainbow veins flap so quickly, too fast for the eye to see, and yet
they leave a noisy trail in their wake. *Bzzzzzzzz* . . . Who knew a
fly made such a sound?

Today is the morning of my fortieth birthday. I lie here in bed,
knowing I should already be up and out, opening the cards
downstairs that have arrived through my letterbox in the last
few days, but instead I pull the duvet up under my chin, prop
myself up on my pillows and continue watching the fly circling
the room.

Fascinating.

There have been too many moments like this to mention over
the last four months since my operation. Slowly the volume on
my implants has been adjusted, and just like I wished all those

years ago as a child, the world has turned up the sound for me.

And what sounds there are. There are simple things like a fly buzzing round my room. Annoying things like the high-pitched whine of a mosquito. Beautiful things like listening to my niece giggle with her friends; and perplexing things: a tap dripping in my bathroom that made me search my house for the sound.

Sound has given me moments I take for granted now, like the fact that I automatically pick up my umbrella from the hallway because my brain has registered the raindrops pitter-pattering on my kitchen roof. There have been times when I've not trusted my new ears to do their work, when I've checked the window, unsure whether to believe that my brain has adjusted well enough to work on automatic without my knowledge. But there they are: giant puddles outside, the rain drip-dropping on the surface and filling them more. So I was right.

There are sounds that I've become accustomed to, like the clink of ice cubes in my glass of cola, and those that can still give me a shock: crunching down on a crisp fresh from a foil bag.

And then there are the sounds that it feels like no amount of time will ever dull the happiness I extract from them: the sound of Mam's voice. That ever-present constant in my life, whose voice feels like a precious gift to me every day.

And then there are the new everyday sounds, the ones I feel excited about that I might hear today.

I jump out of bed and run downstairs to open some gifts, and as I do I'm unprepared for the tearing sounds as I unwrap the paper. I chuckle to myself. And I have got used to hearing my own voice now; it doesn't seem such a stranger to me.

There are still those whose voices I miss, and yet never had the pleasure to hear: Granddad.

But for all those losses, everything I've gained in the last few months has done such a good job of making up for it.

There was my first trip to a classical music concert. I closed my eyes and felt the music flow right through me. There were no words, just pure music. I was in heaven, floating away on a violin or a flute.

Or standing amongst a 50,000-strong crowd at Wembley watching Gateshead FC and hearing 'God Save the Queen' for the first time. The tickets were sent to me by strangers who'd been moved by my story, and I in turn stood amongst the supporters with tears rolling down my cheeks, swept up in patriotism.

My close friends David and Gareth had arranged a trip to see *The Phantom of the Opera* in London. They picked seats which were perfect for my tunnel vision, and I sat mesmerised through the whole thing: the orchestra, the lyrics, the actors . . . an overwhelming and beautiful assault on my senses.

There was even a trip to Las Vegas with Auntie Edna. What an experience: the sights and sounds, the ringing of the fruit machines, the shows, the American accents, the croupiers calling 'no more bets', the roar of the giant water fountains that dance in time to the music outside the Bellagio, and the sound of propellors on our helicipter as we flew over the Grand Canyon.

And sometimes, now I have this incredible sound in my life, it's easier to forget that my sight is still dimming, that each day, though I may not realise it, my tunnel is getting smaller, my view out onto the world shrinking. And the reason it's been so much easier to forget is because of how sound has opened up that tunnel. It's exactly the same as it was, and yet it feels like my vision has doubled.

It is true to say that hearing makes me feel less blind, but in fact I can see less now than I did a year ago. If I did my old Breton-striped top test of years ago today, I'd probably see only my face, perhaps not even my chin now.

And yet, I feel less disabled than I have in years. Yes, I have Usher, yes, I am blind, and yes, I am deaf, and yet what's inside is telling me that this doesn't define or even limit me. The past few months have proved that.

I go to bed with songs ringing in my ears. I wake up and jump into the shower in the morning singing lyrics. I am part of that musical world now.

It hasn't changed the relationships I have with people, except perhaps sometimes I pick up the phone to speak to Mam, or Julie, or Alana now. I'm not confident on the phone, even though I should be able to do it. I feel like I still need to see someone's lips, I still need that prop, that security blanket, but all these things will come in time. I've just got to be patient.

I've had to learn to slow down on building my library of sounds, to actually listen to each new noise, but the temptation is always there to race through as many new sounds as possible, so exciting is my quest to hear everything I've been missing out on for my whole life.

My whole life. Forty years.

I start opening the cards, seeing the wishes of friends who've been with me through my entire journey.

JO MILNE

And there are plenty of celebrations over the next few days as friends get together to celebrate with me. I throw a party at home and friends and family gather in my garden on a sunny Sunday afternoon.

'How about some music?' my friend Richard suggests.

'Ooh yes!' I say; after all, this is the first birthday I've had when I'll actually be able to hear it.

I think back to all those years of Mam giving me the nod as she turned the music down for musical statues, so determined to make me feel included in childhood games. She wouldn't need to now – but there's no need for musical statues today.

And anyway, there is one big problem. I realise I don't own anything to play music on. There's no iPod dock or speakers in a deaf woman's house; it hadn't occurred to me.

My friends rally round, sorting something out, and for the rest of the day we clink glasses and shimmy in time with the music.

Life, for me, really does begin at forty.

In my hands, I am holding a letter from The Osmonds. *The Osmonds*. And yet, I'm standing in my quiet Gateshead kitchen, Matt by my side for company, as I clutch this letter which has travelled all the way across the Atlantic to my little Tyneside semi.

Of course, like most people, I'd known of the American singing family as a child, even if I hadn't heard a single song, but what I didn't know was the story behind them – that of the nine children Olive and George Osmond had, the first two sons were in fact deaf.

The band which filled the *Tops of the Pops* charts for much of

250

the seventies was formed with the sole purpose of buying hearing aids for Virl and Thomas. Even when they went on to greater success, the family remembered the struggle their boys had had and wanted to make sure that no other family struggled like they did to gain access to a hearing world – even more so when Merrill's son, Justin, was born deaf himself.

And so the Olive Osmond Hearing Fund was set up to provide hearing aids for deaf people all over the world, reaching everywhere from Patagonia to Peru.

And here, in this letter now, is a note explaining how the little video of me hearing for the first time had reached this world-famous family in Utah and now they wanted me to be a part of their organisation.

My hands are shaking as I read down the letter.

We would like to offer you a role of ambassador . . .

The tears start pricking at my eyes, blurring the words in front of me.

We feel you would be a positive role model for deaf and deaf-blind people all over the world . . . the letter continues. And my heart is swelling.

I've been feeling for some time that my work at Sense is done. I'd set up the Usher mentoring scheme and I was happy to hand over the reins now, but this . . . This is something else. Not only do I have the chance to help people in the UK, but all over the world.

My job would be to raise funds and awareness so that its work could continue with children in some of the hardest-to-reach places around the globe, that the hearing aids that had allowed me some insight or just the comfort of white noise as a child might benefit a little boy in Ethiopia or a little girl in India, who might otherwise have spent their lives in silence. Not only does the charity provide hearing aids, but also music lessons and speech therapy.

I think back to the years spent sitting with Granddad as he helped me to pronounce capital cities, or Julie miming the words to pop songs while we watched *Top of the Pops* together. I was lucky enough to be born into a family who were happy to spend hours bridging that huge divide between the hearing and deaf world, but I also know not all children are as lucky as me. Not all children realise that they can go out with a disability and be who they want to be, achieve what they want to achieve. And that the loss of one sense – or even two – will not stop them.

And here in my hands is a letter giving me the chance to spread that message around the world.

What on earth would Granddad say? But I didn't really have to ask myself that.

I agreed to my new role without a second thought.

In September 2014, I left all my wonderful colleagues at Sense and started working for the Olive Osmond Hearing Fund. I met Merrill himself, who was in the original group, and his son Justin. And even though our lives had been so different, our stories echoed each other from across the world: a deaf child born to a hearing family who were determined that he wouldn't be treated any differently, that he'd make it into mainstream school, that he'd learn to lip-read rather than sign, and that he'd make the best of what he did have, rather than wishing that life was different.

We shared a TV sofa together to tell our similar stories, and I heard The Osmonds sing at a special concert; something that wouldn't have been possible a year ago.

Would I have believed back then that I would be rubbing shoulders with American singing superstar royalty?

No way. But then, a lot of things have changed in the last year.

A few months ago, I went to a school reunion, and there I bumped into a man who I didn't recognise, though he remembered me. He knew my story from the TV and the newspapers, although that wasn't the reason that he made a beeline for me in the local pub where we'd met for drinks.

'I wanted to say sorry,' he said, shuffling awkwardly and twisting his glass around in his hands.

'What for?' I smiled at him, confused.

And then he told me: he was one of the kids who'd spat on me from the school bus, who'd called me names that I couldn't hear, who'd made animal noises behind my back.

'Do you remember?' he asked, and even though my heart was still stinging with the memories of those cruel taunts and the way I'd have to clean the saliva off my jacket when I got home from school, I looked into his eyes and saw genuine remorse.

'No,' I fibbed, shaking my head. 'We were just kids, I don't remember.'

But he told me how the memories of what he'd said and done to me had followed him round his entire life – and how he was determined that his own kids wouldn't do the same when they came across a disabled child.

'It's made me a better husband, a better father,' he said, guilt stinging his eyes so much that I wanted to do anything to stop him from feeling bad.

But I couldn't take it all away, all I could do was smile and say that it was a million years ago. And it was true: it was. We'd all grown older and wiser with time.

That little deaf girl was gone, and she was replaced by a hearing woman, one who was proud to have Usher and who was determined to go out and make a change in our world, however small, to celebrate our differences rather than punish one another for them.

And then, with pride, I realised that woman was me.

It was a defining moment for me, a time where life had come full circle. Yes, I'd suffered as a result of people like him, but he'd suffered too, and most importantly he'd learnt from it. That was my gift back to him.

My only regret is that I made that decision all those years ago that I didn't want a child of my own. I didn't want them to suffer like me; I'd always been worried to have children in case I passed my condition onto them. But just because I have Usher doesn't mean a child of mine would have it too – the chances are, in fact, very low, or so the doctors tell me – and anyway, I realised then, I was proud to have Usher. Was it such a curse when it had also given me so many gifts?

There are now things like genetic testing and donor eggs for women with Usher who fear having their own child with the condition. And had I learnt more about it twenty years ago then it might have changed the path of my life. I might be writing this now with one of my own children sitting beside me. Being deaf and blind doesn't mean you can't have children, you might just need a little extra help – and that is something I've had to learn to welcome, not fear.

I am also not blind like I'd so feared standing outside that hospital. There is no blackness – not when there will always be some light at the end of my tunnel. It is a lottery. We don't know when my tunnel will stop getting smaller, it could be today, it could be in a year or in ten years, and, yes, there may also be a chance that my vision will shrink to nothing. But while I still have eyes that see in some shape or form, I will use them, cherish them and appreciate every day that I wake up and blink open my eyes to this incredible world.

I always think back to my conversations with Paul at Hunters Moor, and I'll always prefer to have my eyes to see. I've lived forty years of my life being able to see those loved ones around me and I never want to stop seeing them. But I know I could live again in the silent world that I became so accustomed to.

Instead, though, while I have them, I will use my eyes to see places I still want to see, to travel the world, to try new skills. In fact, with the wonderful gift of hearing combined, I plan to learn how to play the piano.

And I have three other amazing senses too: smell, taste, touch. All of these things colour in the picture of our everyday lives. It's only when you've lost one – or two – that you realise just how much.

There have been so many wonderful moments over the last year since I had my implants fitted, yet I still jump a lot at various noises, and there are still sounds that frighten me – the *boom*

boom on firework nights, a car horn when I'm walking down the street, and, yes, I still get caught out by that *crunch* when I eat a packet of crisps!

And while it has been such a wonderful gift to be able to hear, it has also introduced me to a world that isn't as pleasant as I'd thought it was as a deaf woman and, in some ways, I've become a little afraid of it, which wasn't something I felt before.

Now when I walk down the street, it isn't that quiet serene place that I'd assumed. Sometimes I can be amazed at how angry the world is: the impatient drivers who beep their horns, people arguing with each other, things being thrown in a temper, people in a hurry who spit nasty comments if people get in their way, or gangs of kids swearing on a street corner at night. Being deaf, I'd been blissfully unaware of the bad side of sound; after all, I'd never even heard half the names that kids called me at school. Perhaps that had been a blessing.

But now, while I get used to embracing all the *wonderful* sounds around me, I also have to practise blocking out the bad ones, the hate and anger that I hear now.

I suppose, just like when I was a child, I have to refocus on the good and positive things in life: the belly laugh, or a child's giggle, Casey running up to ask me for a biscuit, or my friends sat round a table chatting with me. And Mam.

An incredible gift has been bestowed on me, and I will never take it for granted. Each morning I reach for my implants and turn on a world that is filled with both good and bad.

But I wouldn't have it any other way.

Epilogue

I'm sitting on a busy train. You may have seen me, but chances are I won't have spotted you. That's until you sit down next to me of course. Then I hear the rustle of your paper, smell the coffee in your hand, and I know to turn round and smile at you.

We say hello.

We say something silly about the weather, or make a joke about the story on the front page of your newspaper, and then we get chatting about where each of us works or where we're headed on the train. Our conversation is peppered with laughter as we get to know each other. You stroke Matt who is sitting at my feet, my furry friend who instantly breaks down any barriers that might otherwise have been there.

Suddenly a sound makes me look up. It's a child's giggle ringing out around the carriage. I can see her now, her long white socks and pigtails dancing as she wiggles and squirms in her seat, pointing out all the things to her mam that she can see out of the window.

And as my ears stray further away from our conversation, I notice other things too. A girl chatting excitedly on her mobile phone, planning where to meet her friends for drinks, her newly applied perfume snaking its way through the carriage and hitting my nose. And then there's something else, my favourite sound of all: a man with a deep belly laugh chuckling away at something funny his son has just told him on the phone. My ears lead me to his seat and there he is, clutching his tummy, his shoulders shaking as he attempts to stifle his laughs.

I smile to myself, but instead of turning away to the window, I turn back to my new travelling companion, and we chat on the train all the way home . . .

Playlist

My friend Tremayne created a playlist, An Introduction to Music, which featured a song from every year of my life that I had been without the sense of hearing. These are the songs on the list:

Ken Boothe – Everything I Own
Bruce Springsteen & The E Street Band – She's the One - Live at Hammersmith Odeon
Paul McCartney – Silly Love Songs
Joni Mitchell – Black Crow
Steely Dan – Peg
Electric Light Orchestra – Mr Blue Sky
Gary Numan – Are 'friends' Electric?
The Specials – Do Nothing
Soft Cell – Tainted Love
The Jam – Town Called Malice
Eurythmics – Sweet Dreams (Are Made of This)

Prince – When Doves Cry
Kate Bush – Running Up That Hill (A Deal With God)
The Smiths – Some Girls Are Bigger Than Others
Fleetwood Mac – Big Love - Live (Lindsey Buckingham solo acoustic version)
Tracy Chapman – Fast Car
The The - August & September
Deee-Lite – Groove Is In The Heart
Ozric Tentacles – Sploosh!
INXS – Baby Don't Cry
Nirvana – All Apologies
Richard Thompson – King Of Bohemia
Pulp – Common People - Full Length Version / Album Version
Everything But The Girl – Missing
Foo Fighters – Everlong
Massive Attack – Teardrop
Jimmy Eat World – For Me This Is Heaven
The Avalanches – Frontier Psychiatrist
Daft Punk – Digital Love
The Streets – Turn The Page
Yeah Yeah Yeahs – Maps
Beastie Boys – An Open Letter To NYC
Nine Inch Nails – The Hand That Feeds
Arctic Monkeys – I Bet You Look Good On The Dancefloor
Radiohead - Jigsaw Falling Into Place
Elbow - One Day Like This
Maximo Park – Tanned
Gruff Rhys – Shark Ridden Waters
The Joy Formidable – Whirring
Bat For Lashes – Laura
Haim – Don't Save Me

Acknowledgements

'I would rather walk with a friend in the dark, than alone in the light.'

Helen Keller.

I express my gratitude to all of you who have shared my journey – first and foremost, my family. My parents, Alexander and Ann, my sisters Julie and Alana – blood made us sisters, but our hearts made us friends. My Auntie Edna for being a fun constant throughout and my Auntie Val and Uncle David for always showing love and support. Not forgetting my beautiful niece Casey who never fails to make me smile.

Friends, to all of you. Those from my childhood particularly Victoria and Gillian. From school – too many of you to mention but Emily and Ashfiya who make me feel sweet sixteen again; the friendly neighbourhood of Low Fell and my fellow Geordies;

those I met during those fun growing up years – Sean, Margy, Ray, Kim, Dawn, Zoey and Richard; my work colleagues especially Little Jo; and of course the gang especially the Crossley family, new friends and those I've loved – you have all acquired a disability awareness status simply by sharing your lives with me, which has been an emotional learning curve for us all. It goes a billion miles when one displays compassion, understanding and acceptance to those with Usher Syndrome – we are extraordinary, unique, different people who didn't ask to be deafblind but we are, and like everyone else simply strive to make the best of life and ourselves.

Thank you to my co-writer Anna Wharton – another friend I've been lucky to make in the process of writing this book.

My agent, Diane Banks for her kindness and vision that my story was one to share.

Finally, to my editor Charlotte Hardman – for your helpful advice and for showing such patience, making it a joy and a pleasure to complete my first memoir.